PAINTING AND FINISHING MODELS

This book is due for return on or before the last date shown below.

PAINTING AND FINISHING MODELS

Ian Peacock

ARGUS BOOKS

Argus Books
Argus House
Boundary Way
Hemel Hempstead
Hertfordshire HP2 7ST
England

First published by Argus Books 1987
Reprinted 1989

ISBN 0 85242 912 6

Photosetting by Tradeset Photosetting, Welwyn Garden City.
Printed and bound by LR Printing Services Ltd.
Edward Way, Burgess Hill, West Sussex RH15 9UA, England.

CONTENTS

	FOREWORD	6
1	*PAINTS* Just what are they and what are they made from?	8
2	*EQUIPMENT* All you ever wanted to know about what is needed to apply paints	24
3	*SURFACE PREPARATION* Beauty is only skin deep. Getting the surface right before painting is essential	41
4	*HANDLING PAINTS* Storage, mixing, viscosity, drying times, recoating etc	55
5	*APPLICATION* A guide to masking and application	65
6	*FLYING MODEL AIRCRAFT* A survey of some of the more popular techniques for flying models	79
7	*OTHER WORKING MODELS* Specific problems and their solutions that occur on boats, cars and live steam	91
8	*SMALL SCALE MODELS* Peculiarities in working with small scales. Plastic kits, railways and military figures	103
9	*OTHER ASPECTS* Spin-offs of model painting can lead to other interests	116
	APPENDICES 1–9	121
	INDEX	142

FOREWORD

Everyone has used paint!

It is unusual to be able to start off a new book with a statement that cannot really be contradicted, for at some time or the other everyone *has* used paint. From our first fumblings at primary school with finger painting to adult contretemps with vinyl silk, brush and roller in D.I.Y. household redecoration, paint has become part of our lives. Despite this, many of us have never *really* understood the finer points of paint as a material, nor the complete technical details of its application.

Consequently this book is offered as a stepping stone towards this understanding. It can only ever be a starting point, for much of the expertise demonstrated by experienced exponents of the painting art comes simply from practice, and only with a degree of that time-consuming ingredient firmly beneath one's belt will one achieve the hoped-for results. So go to it. Read, learn, inwardly digest, but above all, practise, for that is what painting is all about!

Just why do we use paint at all? There are three main reasons for painting things.

Environmental Protection A great many artifacts in our modern society stand outside in all weathers. Some form of protection is often required to prevent damage from rust and other corrosion caused by pollutants in the atmosphere – sulphur dioxide, carbon monoxide, acid rain etc., etc. To this end paint is often used as a protection device. We paint the outside of our houses, factories, road and rail bridges and just about any other exterior structure in metal or wood and virtually all forms of transport to try to stave off the ravages of the environment.

Concealment Like the chameleon, whose skin colours change to blend into the surroundings, paint is used widely to achieve something of the same result with man-made structures and machinery. Camouflage is a subject in its own right and government departments spend many hours and much money to come up with colour schemes to make buildings or aircraft and other military vehicles "invisible" to the human eye and hence conceal them from observation.

Adornment Far and above, however, the greatest use stems from the fact that *homo sapiens* appreciates artifacts that are "easy on the eye" and therefore almost every possession is coloured in one form or another. One would not consider painting one's house/car/model or what have you with, say, a protective finish, if it did not "look" attractive. Colour sells! Therefore every manufacturer trying to get his slice of the market will offer colour as an incentive. "This year's colour" is a powerful influence on the potential customer and few are known to resist it. Consequently "Joe Modeller" is faced with the use of colour from every aspect of everyday life.

In the model world there is often need to colour a chosen example to emulate the "real thing", whether it is a camouflaged military vehicle or a bright and colourful ceremonial military uniform. In other areas, there may be need for specific environmental protection (e.g. in fuel-proofing a power-driven model to reduce the likelihood of chemical attack on the surface) or for specialist finishes such as heat-resistant paints on "live steam" models. In general, however, it is probably true to say that most of us have only the decorative aspect in mind.

Whichever category *you* fall into, nothing is more certain than that ultimately the need for paint and the knowledge of how to apply it properly will require your attention.

1   PAINTS

Historically it is difficult to be exact about the origin of painting. Certainly the ancient Chinese knew about lacquers, both for decorative/ artistic purposes and as a protective finish. So it is probable that "paints" were in use more than 2000 years ago. Up until the middle 1900s paints were made from natural products, some colours giving a clue to the origins of these natural items. Vermilion, Saffron, Terracotta, Burnt Umber are all to be found in the better class artist's palettes. More recently, synthetic resins, developed for a variety of chemical requirements, have all but taken over the paint manufacturing industry, providing the end user with a multitude of benefits. More startling colours, better weather protection, longer lasting colours less prone to fading, easier methods of application (non-drip paints etc.) are all end-user benefits.

Today's products provide the modeller with a degree of choice unthought of by previous generations. Despite this there is a marked reluctance by most modellers to experiment, not only with newer types of paints, but also with established lines of colouring media "not normally" associated with our hobby.

It would be a great help to us all if we could neatly "pigeon-hole" different types of paints, from the point of view of reference, in positively-named categories. However, many manufacturers refer to their products by a variety of generic terms such as "enamel" or "lacquer" which are blatantly contradictory of technical fact or traditional acceptance and can therefore lead the unwary into deep trouble. Nevertheless, a basic understanding of paint types *will* enable the hobbyist to be at least part way prepared to tackle the veritable jungle of commercially-available finishing media.

Enamels
As a generalisation, enamels are oil-bound paints of the sort more "usually" associated with painting plastic kits and which are widely available through the retail hobby outlets in small jars or tinlets of around half ounce or so capacity. Names like HUMBROL, established

many years ago, and more recently PRECISION PAINTS and D.B.I. come readily to mind.

The vast majority of enamels consist of a carrier lacquer made up of a mixture of natural oils and resins (often referred to as "clear varnish") to which is added the colour. Colour addition is by means of a

Scores of different colours are available in the world-renowned Humbrol range of ½-ounce tinlets, in both gloss and matt finish. Many are also packed in small aerosols or special purpose selections.

finely ground pigment. Originally all coloured pigments were from natural substances but today many synthetic pigments are used. The fine grinding of the pigment has a great deal to do with the end quality of the paint, and pigment ground to a consistency better than face powder is not uncommon. The materials for pigmentation are insoluble solids and in order that they can be carried in the clear varnish by "suspension" it is necessary to reduce the solid to an even and minuscule particle size. Pigments suitable for most modelling enamels will be ground to a particle size of less than half a micron. (A micron is approximately 39 millionths of an inch.) The small size of these particles allows them to "float" suspended in the clear carrying medium for the duration of their immediate use, but as they do not actually dissolve, they will eventually sink to the bottom. This settling out process causes the majority of the painting problems, as few modellers take adequate steps to ensure a good "mix" before use. (More of this in Chapter 4.)

During paint manufacture, there are many types of grinding systems used to break down the lumps of pigment to this small, uniform size. Larger particles, rotated in a drum, will grind against each other, aided by the addition of suitable liquid lubricants, much as pebbles on the beach are reduced by the constant action of the tide.

Agitators

Steel balls may be introduced to the drum, which as it rotates causes the balls to "climb up" the side of the drum, tumbling back into the mixture of pigment and lubricant. The constant tumbling action causes the pigments to be broken down into small particles. There are other versions of machinery that achieve the same effect, one of which replaces the steel balls with a special kind of sand. Agitation is usually provided by motor driven paddles which again cause the pigment to break down into small particles.

One other major technique is the high speed dispenser, working much like the driven paddles but at much higher speed. Replacing the paddles is a "dispersion head" not unlike a milling cutter, whose teeth, rotating at speeds of up to 10,000 rpm, literally cut the particles down to size. As one can imagine, the action of this sort of machine is somewhat violent.

The "clear varnish" part of paint is a fair bit more complex than its title suggests and it usually consists of the base carrier modified by the addition of driers, solvents, plasticisers etc. to offer the user good all-round performance. In practice, most paints of the enamel family dry moderately quickly to a high gloss and additional "flatting" agents are introduced to provide the matt camouflage effect much sought after by the military modelling brigade.

Once more, as a generalisation, modelling enamels can be used "straight from the can" when new (after suitable stirring!) but if thinning is required, then "white spirit" or turps substitute is the most commonly used medium. Some manufacturers expressly recommend their own particular brand of thinner – usually at some elevated price. This is not usually a simple case of "ripping off the punter" for there is a variety of very sophisticated thinning agents available to the manufacturer today and it is not unusual to find that a blend of these additives has been specially created to allow a better surface finish, quicker drying, or other "end user" advantages to be passed on.

Availability is the biggest advantage of enamel paints. Literally hundreds of thousands of small jars and tins are sold every year and the colour range, often matched to an original shade with painstaking accuracy, is vast. Now I *know* that colour matching to the "real thing" does not necessarily make for a perfect appearance in model form and much has been written on the effect of "reducing" scale colour (see Chapter 4 for more on this subject!) but to the vast majority of modellers, the colour on the can is the colour on the model!

Against this ready availability is the fact that while half an ounce goes a long way in 1/72nd scale it hardly dents the surface in the larger scales of, say 7¼in. gauge locomotives or quarter-scale radio-controlled model aircraft. Having to buy a half a gross of tinlets to cover a 9ft wingspan *Spitfire* or a 5½ft long *Flying Scotsman* would be ludicrous; most makers supply larger tins (even if only 2oz.) but these larger quantities do not appear to be so widely stocked and may therefore entail something of a search.

Cellulose

High on the list of finishing materials in all aspects of industry and right behind enamel is nitro-cellulose lacquer (sometimes referred to in the trade as synthetic automobile enamel – which is enough to confuse anyone!). Derived originally from the explosive "gun cotton", cellulose material in solid form, known as celluloid, and for a long time one of the first of the "plastics", was around in the late 19th century. Dissolving celluloid in amyl acetate or one of the alcohols produced the first cellulose lacquers or "dope". Cellulose dries purely by the evaporation of the solvent to leave a thin, hard, clear film that is somewhat brittle. The rapid evaporation of the solvents, particularly when compared with the evaporation of the oils in enamel paints, is a mixed blessing, for little time is available to allow brush marks to flow out and

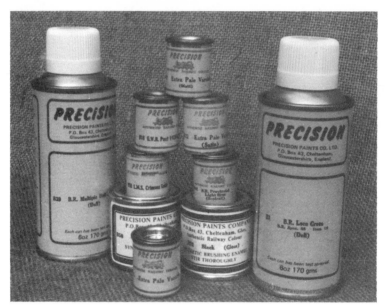

Precision Paints are well respected in the U.K., especially among railway modellers. U.S. equivalent is Floquil.

therefore cellulose is usually better sprayed. Against this, its more rapid drying leaves it less susceptible to the settlement of dust onto its wet surface. The brittle nature of cellulose may be easily overcome and the addition of plasticisers is now commonplace. To increase the flexibility still further, many aeromodellers add an egg cup full of medicinal castor oil to every quart of clear dope.

Many chemicals can be added to cellulose, apart from colour pigments, to result in a good colour coverage, and long, fade-free life without embrittlement. Unlike enamels, the lack of availability is the major stumbling block for modellers. No longer is the half-ounce tinlet the obvious route. The days when one could buy matt camouflage dopes in the friendly neighbourhood model shop have long since gone. The paints *are* still manufactured and *are* still widely available, although not from the model shop and not in half-ounce tins! The route to go here is to visit the specialist suppliers to the motor refinishing trade (or to shop from advertising specialist colour dope suppliers). Although much of the motor trade has moved over to acrylic finishes, cellulose is still widely used, and probably will be for many a long year to come. Its availability is generally limited to cans of around a litre, although some local stockists can have their arm twisted to sell the odd half litre to the impecunious model maker. In terms of colours, well, the current trend in the motor industry is toward computer matching from stock shades. Most stockists will have a shade book with upward of 5000 colour samples. Each sample will have a hole or window in it through which one can view. The secret here is to purchase a half-ounce tin or jar of the exact colour-matched enamel and apply some to a piece of white card. When dry, trot along to your stockist and slide the sample card beneath the relevant page of the colour book, moving the sample from window to window until the shades match. From here on it becomes only a question of parting with money!

Cellulose is probably the easiest of all paints to apply by spray within the limits of an amateur environment, and further details of application techniques will be found in Chapter 5 and subsequent chapters on "special" disciplines.

Thinners

Unlike enamels, cellulose can rarely be applied "straight from the can" and therefore the use of thinner is virtually mandatory. Cellulose thinner is very volatile, evaporates rapidly and is highly inflammable. Consequently, all references to safety should be rigidly adhered to.

"Special" thinners are often used for specific reasons. "Slow" thinners will slow the drying time and "non-bloom" thinners are of particular use when excess dampness in the atmosphere causes white patches on the drying surfaces.

Apart from thinners, there are often advantages to using special additives to cellulose (and in some cases to other paints as well – check with the paint manufacturers for data sheets and compatibility). Accelerated additives, sometimes incorporated in "fast" or "cold weather" thinners can, as their name suggests, speed up drying time when the ambient conditions are cold. That does not mean, however, that one can paint in sub-zero temperatures.

Other additives of benefit to the modeller can often be obtained from motor factors. "Softening" or "flexing" additives are now in widespread use for painting the plastic and glass fibre parts of modern motor vehicles. Usually clear in colour, they can be added to both cellulose and acrylics (make sure you get the correct additive for your kind of paint – they are not all interchangeable!) in amounts of up to 50%. The result is a paint that will absorb flexing without cracking. Matting agents can also be obtained, their use being somewhat self explanatory.

Various comments are regularly expounded about the areas of use of cellulose but the most important of these is that cellulose paints *should not* be applied over many plastics (including the styrene from which plastic kits are made) or over models already finished or part finished with enamel or other oil-based paints. The powerful solvents contained in cellulose paints will seriously affect the plastic or enamel base and can easily ruin the model. Of course all generalisations of this nature can be disproved in specific circumstances and just which circumstances will be fully covered later in the book.

The main disadvantage with a cellulose finish concerns motor-driven models, particularly where the motor is of the glow-plug variety, for the hot exhaust waste from these motors attacks cellulose very quickly and severely. Consequently a surface coating of some suitable fuel-proof lacquer will be required *after* painting and decorating. Once more, every cloud has a silver lining and if the final fuel-proof coat is either gloss or matt to suit the overall required effect, then it matters little whether the colour coats are matt, gloss or anywhere in between.

Butyrates

Some years ago, in an attempt to provide the modeller with a "fuel proof dope" there was a move toward producing a synthetic cellulose which was based upon butyrates rather than the traditional nitrates of cellulose. To a large extent butyrate based colours have now died out for they were found to be not so fuel resistant in practice as they seemed to be under laboratory conditions. Coupled with this was the problem that nitrate and butyrate based products are not normally compatible with each other leading to all sorts of end-user problems. Butyrate dope could not be mixed with nitrate dope nor could the respective thinners be interchanged. Furthermore, difficulties were often experienced with multiple coats for second coat application with butyrate based products could not be achieved in anything like as short a time as with "normal" cellulose. To make matters worse, many modellers were prone to using one colour in nitrate and a contrasting colour in butyrate, leading to the well known problem of "pickling" should the nitrate be applied over the butyrate. If all this was not enough to put people off, additional fuel proofing over mixed finishes was also fraught with disaster.

Although all but disappeared from the modelling market, various forms of synthetic celluloses have sprung upon the motor vehicle trade, and can, with care, be used for modelling. Their advantages are often in the ease of application, their general cleanliness and a reduced hazard to health. Try them – they work! But do check carefully the compatibility with the base material and the effect that over-coating with fuel might have.

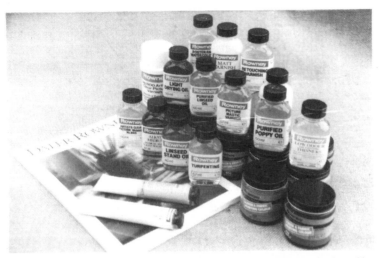

Product line from Daler-Rowney. Many types of artists' paints can be found in this type of manufacturer's catalogue. Note the vast range of varnishes, oils and modifiers.

Acrylics

Perspex or Plexiglas is an acrylic, but in terms of paint composition the acrylic is a tough, shiny, synthetic resin that, given the right solvents, can be rendered liquid. This simple statement covers up a really complex chemical business, for acrylics as applied to paints are not too easy to pigeon-hole.

A large number of modern motor vehicle paints are of the acrylic family, many having brilliant colours with a greater resistance to fading than either cellulose or enamels. Once more, its own specialist and highly volatile solvents and thinners make it difficult to apply by brush. Like cellulose, it polishes well and is resistant to a large number of today's chemicals (although it is not fuel-proof).

The amateur sprayer should experience no difficulty in applying acrylics.

Now here comes the rub. Some acrylics are a "single pack" product, i.e. like enamels and cellulose, they come in a single can and dry by a combination of the rapid evaporation of the solvents combined with a small amount of chemical action within the paint itself.

Where the problem really occurs is that there are other forms of acrylics in widespread use. One of these is a two-pack product. This, as its name suggests, comes packed in two cans, one containing the pigmented resin and the other the catalytic hardening agent. The resins will not naturally air-harden in this instance and rely on intermixing with the correct volume of the hardener or activator to begin a "curing" process which is largely a chemical action. True, there is still some evaporation of the solvents and thinners but the major factor with two-pack paints is the chemical change brought about during the curing process. Two-part acrylics exhibit a surface shine above average and a surface toughness that surpasses most modelling requirements. (For instance, it is proof against most chemicals, including hot fuels and exhaust waste!) It is easy to apply by brush or spray and flows out smoothly without runs or snags. Availability is typical of what might be expected of a motor refinishing industry product. Like single pack acrylics it demands its own special thinners.

If it is as good as all that, why are we not all using it? Well, everything has two sides and the snag with most of these products is the health hazard. Of course, most paints of the volatile solvent variety are a potential hazard and this is dealt with more fully elsewhere. However, many of the two-pack acrylics contain cyanide as one of the constituents of the hardener. Quite obviously, breathing in too many fumes can seriously shorten one's modelling career!

Inhalation Risks
Industrially the use of these paints is heavily frowned upon, save in specially prepared spray booths and with the operators wearing proper breathing equipment. Despite this, many small-time operators

One of the first and now the most widely used two-pack epoxy paints are the Hobbypoxy range from the U.S.A. See appendix for intermixing details. Note that special thinner is necessary.

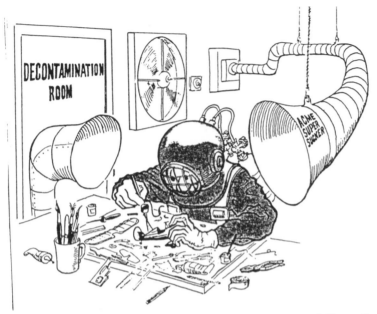

"... breathing in too many fumes can seriously shorten one's modelling ..."

use these paints and appear to get away with it. The problem is we do not know what long-term effects these fumes have on the lining of the lungs. Certainly those users who already suffer from chest and lung ailments come down rapidly with only short exposure to the fumes and readers are advised to proceed along this route with caution and awareness of the nature of the problems.

Other forms of acrylic have appeared recently that are water-based. Such products have been developed as offshoots of the D.I.Y. trade and are often seen in use in Junior schools where the ability to remove "wet" paint with copious amounts of water is a major bonus.

Not really falling into the "water colour" pigeon hole, these paints have a definite position within our hobby for they are extremely flexible and have excellent adhesion, making them eminently suitable for application on the flexible plastics from which small scale model soldiers are made.

Polyesters
Polyesters are not normally associated with painting. However, various subvariants of the polyester families *do* crop up in model making. The most widespread use is in the production of glass-fibre parts for models, aircraft fuselages and boat hulls being two such examples to spring to mind. Quite often pigmented resins are used to *avoid* the

need for subsequent painting. Other versions of these resins can be used for certain types of surface preparation and this is covered more fully in Chapter 3.

Polyesters are once more non-air drying substances and require the addition of a hardener to effect the necessary chemical change (referred to as polymerisation) to bring about a cure to a rigidly glass-like surface. Polyesters do however contain powerful solvents and can easily melt certain base materials. Discoloration with age is not normally a problem with these resins which, when fully cured, exhibit good surface resistance to many solvents, are heat resistant to a degree and have a very high gloss.

Epoxides

Epoxy resins are another modern synthetic finish that have much to commend them in certain specific applications. They have a marked increase in adhesion, an excellent gloss, extremely good flexibility and exhibit particularly good rejection of attack by organic chemicals (i.e. they are fuel-proof).

Epoxy resin adhesives have been with us for many years yet epoxy paints have been slow to catch on in the modelling world. Despite this, industry has been quick to seize upon their advantages and much industrial finishing is now done with these paints. Epoxides are, in general, two part products but *do not* contain cyanide. Once more, only the specially formulated thinning agents should be used. Cure is a mixture of evaporation of the contained solvents and chemical reformulation. Like most paints of this type, chemical cure can be advanced by the application of gentle heat and slowed down in cold weather. Epoxides are, by and large, carcenogenic (i.e. cancer forming) and much alarmist concern has been put across in print. However, used with reasonable caution and some sensible safety measures, the occasional use under amateur conditions is not likely to be serious.

Because of the two part nature, storage, once mixed, is of limited time. However, this can be extended by storing mixed paints in the 'fridge.

Colour mixing can, however, be achieved (and stored for considerable periods!) before addition of the hardener.

For the camouflage addicts, accurate mixing charts are provided by some manufacturers (Hobbypoxy for instance) and both gloss and flat hardeners are on offer. In fact clear epoxy – and for that matter other two part paints – mixed with the relevant hardener, makes an excellent fuel-proof finish to apply, say, over a cellulose base.

Polyurethane

Like acrylics, polyurethanes may be a one-pack product, polymerisation occurring purely through oxidisation in the atmosphere, or a two-pack catalytic cured system.

Two-pack urethanes act in many ways like acrylics and epoxides in as much as a chemical change takes place upon mixing and that special thinners are required. The resulting coat is extremely hard-wearing with good resistance to abrasion, corrosion and weathering, indeed it is fuel-proof. However, the activator reacts to water and therefore some care needs to be taken during manufacture, storage and application.

Single-pack urethanes are much more akin to enamel and do not have such high properties as the two-pack varieties. Single-pack clear polyurethane, for example, is neither fuel-proof nor abrasion-resistant to the same extent. Furthermore, clear, single-pack urethanes yellow badly with age (as in fact do many oil bound clear lacquers).

"Yacht varnish" is often a two pack urethane product and ships chandlers are usually worth a visit if you have difficulty finding a source of supply.

Powermax POLYKOTE – a range of modern polymer paints (gloss and matt) much favoured by the larger scale flying modellers as they are easy to apply and are claimed to be fuel-proof. Paints available in much larger tins (and aerosols) to suit this end of the market. Note that multi polymer paints of this type *must* be used with their own thinner. Primer/undercoat is a different polymer and has its own thinner (not to be confused with that for the paint). Thinners must not be interchanged.

Many household paints are single pack urethanes and there are a myriad of offshoots of this form of polymer chemistry. Powermax paints, much favoured by the scale model aircraft brigade, are just such an offshoot, having quite complex chemical formulation. Very often paints such as this use the oxygen in the atmosphere to create the catalisation. Consequently they are usually canned in a nitrogen atmosphere to aid shelf life, polymerisation commencing when the tin is first opened.

Stoving Paints

There are many variants of both natural and synthetic resins that exhibit a tendency to stay "tacky" at room temperatures, yet go quite hard (extremely hard in fact) if raised to an elevated temperature. Stoving enamels are widely used in many aspects of industry and can in fact be used by the hobbyist. However, the requirement of a stoving oven tends to put their use outside of all but the dedicated enthusiast. Constructing such an oven is not too difficult but presupposes that one has spraying and stoving facilities *outside* of one's dwelling place, as well as a reasonably good standard of engineering. Furthermore the cost is such that it would be necessary to do quite a bit of this type of painting to reap any real benefit. It if *does* become necessary to use stoving paints for specific model jobs, then it is probably going to be easier (and probably quicker and cheaper) to contact a local specialist to do the work for you.

STOVING OVENS

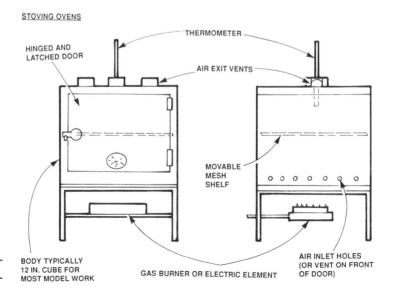

HINGED AND LATCHED DOOR

THERMOMETER

AIR EXIT VENTS

MOVABLE MESH SHELF

BODY TYPICALLY 12 IN. CUBE FOR MOST MODEL WORK

GAS BURNER OR ELECTRIC ELEMENT

AIR INLET HOLES (OR VENT ON FRONT OF DOOR)

Apart from their hardness, the other prime benefit with stoving paints is their resistance to elevated temperature. (There are a few specialised single pack, brushable, air-drying paints that exhibit high temperature resistance, but they do tend to be amongst the very specialised industrial products.)

Live steam railway fans differ widely in their recommendation here, many stating that paints used on boilers should stand up to 150°C and more. Others argue, quite correctly, that if a boiler is suitably lagged conventional oil bound or cellulose paints will do, keeping the stoving paints for the fire box and smoke box, both of which are usually black.

Water Colours

Water-based artist's colours and inks are not widely used within the model world for no good reason that I can find.

Traditionally we all think of "paint" with which to finish our models. Yet if we take a sports type radio-controlled aircraft as an example there is no real reason why ink, water colour, or even the ubiquitous felt tip pens cannot be favourably employed.

Assuming that white cellulose primer has been used as a pre-finish (see Chapter 3) then the overall surface will be very akin to a good quality art paper or card. The use of water based colorants is quick and easy and the thinner/cleaner is cheap! A final spray coat of one of the proprietary fuel-proofing agents will effectively seal in the colour from the ravages of the outside world.

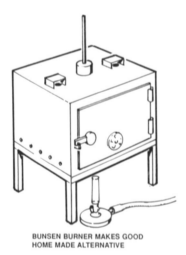

BUNSEN BURNER MAKES GOOD
HOME MADE ALTERNATIVE

Humbrol produce a variety of specialised paints, most of which are oil-based and some of which are displayed in this photograph.

While dwelling briefly on the subject of water colours mention should be made of:

Fabric Dyes

Not strictly a model finishing medium, but one that might well fit into associated crafts.

Fabric dyes are available suited to both brush or spray application. Their use in model-making is limited but the creation of lozenge patterned fabric to cover a flying model of a W.W.1 German fighter is not only authentic but a great deal lighter than using a paint. For my part, I have taken a delight in using these dyes to produce model-associated products such as club sweatshirts with emblems or badges applied via stencil to produce a simple, cheap and effective corporate image.

Finally in this chapter we must not overlook a specialised synthetic resin widely used by aircraft and power boat operators alike.

Tufkote

Tufkote is a U.K. offshoot of the furniture industry and was originally marketed as "Furniglass Hardset". Now manufactured by the Evode conglomerate, it is no longer available as a furniture finish but *is* available via the majority of U.K. model and hobby retailers. It is melamine-reinforced urea-formaldehyde and is a two-part acid-cured resin. It may be readily thinned with either cellulose thinner or methylated spirit (not usually more than 20%) for spraying. Like most two-part lacquers it dries to a high gloss, is totally fuel-proof and does not yellow with age.

Tufkote can be applied by brush but it is far better sprayed. The powerful solvents can easily soften the paint coat beneath, causing colour to "drag" with the brush. One well-known colleague produced a superb red and white chequer-board Pitts Special biplane and fuel-proofed it with a brush! Result – red and *PINK* chequer-boards!

The original TUFKOTE has been replaced with NEW Tufkote due to rationalisation of the company products.

NEW Tufkote is basically the same, but with changes to the hardener (acid curing agent). The original product had a somewhat vigorous curing agent that was easy to use, but hazardous from the health point of view. The New version has a safer curing system. Of course, nothing ever comes for free, and reduction of the hazard has brought increase in curing time. No longer can one recoat after a couple of hours – (the norm with the old Tufkote) – but, dependent upon temperature, a minimum of 48 hours is needed to effect sufficient cure to avoid pickling with re-coating.

In many ways similar to Tufkote is another British product, Aerokote. Aerokote has the advantage of being available in both gloss and matt finishes and is also a two part, acid cured system. Here too, the less aggressive curing agent results in much longer time taken between coats, a problem that does not endear it to modellers.

To summarise, therefore, most single-part paints air dry by evaporation or oxidisation. Most two-part paints effect a chemical change during cure and this may well be accompanied by evaporation. Drying times vary and the problem of drying time as applied to multiple coats is covered in Chapter 4.

In general, use only new cans of paint and try not to mix brands. Avoid if at all possible using one type of paint on top of another. If you have to follow this route – and you may have no choice – then experiment *first* on some scrap material to test for compatibility. Failure to do this could lead to a costly recovering exercise at best and a totally ruined model at worst.

2 EQUIPMENT

There can be no doubt in anyone's mind that the use of an airbrush or spray gun in competent hands will provide a quality of surface finish unequalled by any other form of paint application. Were this not so, motor cars, washing machines and many other articles would still be brush painted.

In the hands of the enthusiastic amateur, even modest spray equipment can achieve near miracles, yet despite this many never aspire to its use. There are several reasons for this, cost being the predominant factor. Good painting equipment does not come cheaply and any attempt to short-cut the financial aspect will certainly reduce the end result. The other major stumbling block is the fear generated by lack of knowledge. It is now more than ten years since I gave my first lecture on the principles and uses of spraying equipment, yet even today I am regularly approached by modellers asking the same old questions.

So if many are still put off spraying, then an equal number must still use the ubiquitous paint-brush! Even here one *must* spend money, for only the very best paint-brushes are of sufficient quality for good modelling work.

Brushes
Most experts agree that natural hair brushes will be better than artificial hair for the majority of painting work. Despite this, great strides have been made in recent years in developing synthetic materials for the manufacture of paint-brushes and in certain cases it could be argued that the modern synthetic has much to offer.

Traditionally sable hair is used for the finest of high quality brushes and Kolinsky sable is probably the tops. The very best sable brushes are made from the highly resilient tail hair of the wild mink, a species of weasel found only in the intensely cold climates of Siberia and North Korea. For paint-holding capacity there is no better natural fibre. The extreme rarity of the hair is the prime cause of the high cost of this sort of paint-brush and from time to time the larger sizes of brush be-

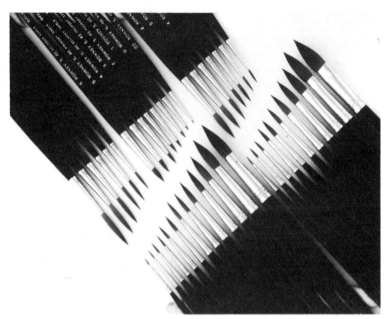

The best you can get. A selection of Kolinsky sable artists' brushes from the Rowney range.

come difficult to acquire. Sable hair brushes come in an assortment of styles and sizes which vary from brand to brand. Sizes are "graded" with the lower numbers representing the smaller brushes and larger numbers (12–14 being amongst the biggest) representing larger brushes. Most fine art brushes are circular in cross section tapering to a very fine point. Varying manufacturers and styles will offer longer or

Dalon synthetic bristle brushes from Daler of Daler-Rowney, available in most standard shapes and some extra-small sizes.

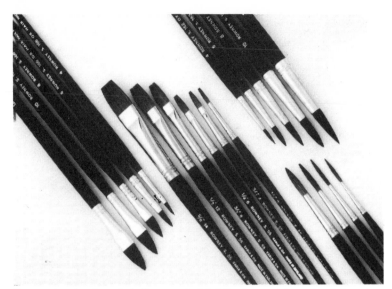

Rowney brushes in ox hair (the very dark bristles) or a mixture of ox hair and sable, in all usual sizes.

shorter hairs to suit individual tastes. In general terms, the longer haired brushes are preferred by signwriters and lining artists and make the best choice for general modelling.

Other shapes are also valid: the flat or chisel pointed brush is better for larger areas and some manufacturers even produce combination types where they "appear" pointed when dry but change to a chisel end when loaded with paint.

Probably the best alternative to sable is Dalon. Dalon is a man-made fibre which is a remarkable imitation of natural sable. Each synthetic filament is extruded to a fine point just like natural hair and construction of the brush head (ferrule) is meticulously hand-crafted to the same standards as the "real" sable brushes. Dalon's high resilience and durability ensure excellent shape retention and long life in the less than perfect use that they might well find in the hands of modellers. The resulting cost reduction also makes them an attractive product. Once more a wide choice of sizes and styles may be had (in fact artificial hair brushes are often found in much smaller sizes than natural sable!) and some of the larger flat shapes are ideal for painting larger models.

More economic are brushes made from the hair of ox, squirrel, goat and ring-cat and it is not uncommon to find brushes of mixed hair.

Nylon and other man-made fibres are now widely used and can offer further cost savings.

Thirteen Grumbacher brushes shown approximately actual size. From the bottom up the sizes are 000, 00, 0, 1, 2, 3, 4, 5, 6, 7, 8, 10 and 12. Flat one-stroke and poster brushes are sized by width in inches or millimetres.

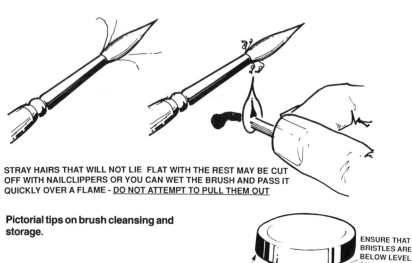

STRAY HAIRS THAT WILL NOT LIE FLAT WITH THE REST MAY BE CUT OFF WITH NAILCLIPPERS OR YOU CAN WET THE BRUSH AND PASS IT QUICKLY OVER A FLAME - <u>DO NOT ATTEMPT TO PULL THEM OUT</u>

Pictorial tips on brush cleansing and storage.

KEEP BRUSHES CLEAN AND STORE WITH BRISTLES NOT TOUCHING ANYTHING!

CONVERT OLD CARDBOARD BOX BY ADDING CROSS PIECE PUNCHED WITH HOLES. STORE HANDLE END DOWN TO PREVENT BRISTLE TOUCHING OTHER END OF BOX

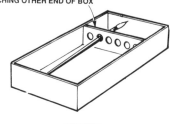

CLOSE FITTING LID

ENSURE THAT BRISTLES ARE BELOW LEVEL OF LID AND ABOVE CARD SUPPORT

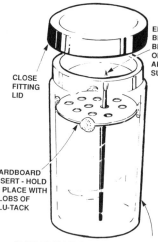

CARDBOARD INSERT - HOLD IN PLACE WITH BLOBS OF BLU-TACK

GLASS OR PLASTIC KITCHEN CONTAINER

METHOD 1   METHOD 2

PULL BRUSH THIS WAY

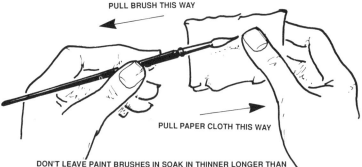

PULL PAPER CLOTH THIS WAY

DON'T LEAVE PAINT BRUSHES IN SOAK IN THINNER LONGER THAN NECESSARY. WHEN DRYING CLEAN BRUSHES USE PAPER TOWEL RATHER THAN CLOTH AND WIPE ONLY AWAY FROM FERRULE - NEVER WIPE BRISTLES TOWARD FERRULE

Hog's hair (sometimes known as pig's bristle) brushes are also widely available to the artist market. These brushes are somewhat stiffer than natural sable or its synthetic equivalent and have not the same widespread use in modelling. However, model painting is a "horses for courses" area and the idea that one product will cover all eventualities is definitely fallacious. Stiff pig's bristle brushes come into their own when working with clear dope and similar lacquers on open weave fabric: i.e. nylon covering on open-framed aircraft structures, for example. Here there is need not only to cover the fabric with the clear dope, but to work it well into the weave of the fabric. Any "scrubbing" action to achieve this end will surely damage a soft hair brush beyond sensible repair, but the stiffness and springiness of hog's hair will take this in its stride.

Paint-brushes should be looked after more carefully than any other modelling tool. They are expensive to buy but if maintained and stored correctly they will last a lifetime. *Never* store paint-brushes in a manner that can damage their hairs. Store them either upright or lying down in a closed container. Protect the hairs by fitting a small tube over the end of the brush. Offcuts of drinking straws will suffice for the smaller sizes and other bits of plastic tube (left-over fuel tube or heat-shrink from electrical jobs) can be pressed into service for the larger sizes.

Scrupulous cleanliness will pay dividends. Clean up immediately after use and don't leave the brush propped up in a jar of thinners overnight. When thoroughly clean, point up the hairs to the natural

Left, brushes with reasonably thick handles can be drilled and suspended on a piece of wire. Other methods (below) are jamming the handles into holes drilled in a strip of wood or punched in a jar lid. In any event such suspension should only be on a temporary basis.

shape and pay particular attention to the ferrule to ensure that there is no paint build-up at the root of the hairs. If stored for a long time, use an airtight container (I use a Tupperware spaghetti pot!) to avoid any build-up of mildew or moth grub attack.

Cleaning
Use the correct thinner for cleaning, although it is permissible to use more aggressive thinner for very stubborn cases. Cellulose thinner, amyl acetate or methyl ethyl ketone (MEK for short) can be used to remove most paints. Take special care when cleaning after using *any* of the two-pack resin paints, for these form tenacious bonds when cured and cannot be softened with the current crop of easily-available solvents. Two-pack paints *must* be cleaned out *while still wet*.

It if becomes imperative that brushes should be left in soak for any period of time, they should be suspended from their handles in such a way that the bristles/hairs do not touch the sides or bottom of the solvent container. Many modellers simply drill a small hole through the handle and push a piece of wire through to support the brush on the edges of the top of the container. Others, not wishing to damage the brush handle, use other tricks. Soft wire wound spirally round the handle works well. So will a couple of strips of *hard* 3/16in. square balsa, elastic banded together, with the brush handle passed between them. Many would say that it pays to keep paint-brushes for specific jobs or for specific paints, labelling up the handles for reference, rather than using any old brush for any old job. Although this will increase the financial outlay, the long term availability of brushes so used will probably justify the exercise.

In general, it will pay to use the largest brush that you can, commensurate with the area to be painted. The application of a coat of paint should be thin and this is where the softness and mass of the sable type brush will score. Stiff bristles will cause the paint to furrow like a ploughed field. For paint to flow out and for brush marks to disappear it is essential that the film of paint remains unbroken and that the surface tension is maintained. It is this surface tension that evens out the peaks and troughs in the paint to produce the smooth final surface. Too much "furrowing" will break up the uniformity of the paint and destroy the surface tension, leaving the peaks and troughs to dry where they are. Wherever possible work with the brush "laid low" to reduce the angle between the hairs and the painted surface and apply the first charged brush stroke along the longest direction of the model. Follow by brushing out across the initial path and, finally, very lightly stroke over the surface in the original direction.

One of the most famous names in airbrushes is Aerograph-de Vilbiss. This is their Super 63 model, capable of any fine modelling work.

Airbrushes and Spray Guns

Spray painting is a horse of a different colour. Once more it is apparent that a large number of manufacturers offer an even larger number of variants within their range. Specific choice of airbrush or spray gun will be up to the individual, bearing in mind the type and size of model that requires painting. As a general guide, working models, i.e. live steam locos, radio control 'planes and boats will benefit from the acquisition of a small spray gun – possible from the automotive touch up business – or a "large" airbrush. Modellers working in smaller scales, "OO" railways, 1/72nd scale plastics etc., will be far better off with the artists' size airbrush. Much has been written in magazines on the subject of airbrushing but there is little in book form of direct use to modellers and the more serious enthusiast would do well to obtain a copy of my previous book (*Airbrushing and Spray Painting Manual*, published by Argus Books) which covers this ground in much greater depth. Sufficient here therefore to look in broad generalities at the problems besetting the would-be beginner to spraying.

Spraying in the smaller scales demands an airbrush. This is just a sophisticated name for a miniature spray gun with a minuscule nozzle and which is often the shape of a propelling pencil or ball-point pen. Minute quantities of paint, properly thinned, are needed and these are contained either in small jars slung beneath the airbrush or in small cups fitted to the top of the forebody or plugging into its side. The action of the airbrush is to expel compressed air from the front of the jet or nozzle, which carries with it the finely atomised paint onto the model in a smooth, even and thin coating.

Airbrushes, by design, fall roughly into three categories. The first and usually the best (from the performance point of view and also from the elevated cost) is roughly defined as "Double Action – Needle controlled". Control of this type of airbrush is by virtue of a single control button usually mounted on top of the forebody. This button has two functions, up and down controlling the air flow and backwards and forwards controlling the paint flow, by way of a precision tapered needle within the body. This is where the airbrush gets its name. This type of control offers the user the greatest possible flexibility, enabling paint to be faded in or out during use and allowing delicate shading and ultra fine lines to be produced, all at the control of one's index finger.

HOME MADE SPRAY BOOTH

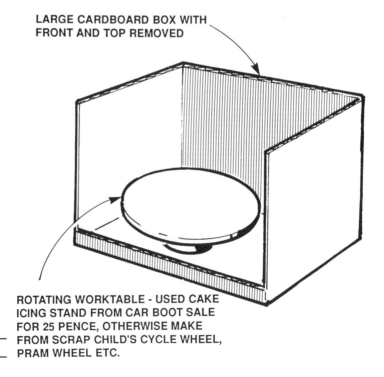

LARGE CARDBOARD BOX WITH
FRONT AND TOP REMOVED

ROTATING WORKTABLE - USED CAKE
ICING STAND FROM CAR BOOT SALE
FOR 25 PENCE, OTHERWISE MAKE
FROM SCRAP CHILD'S CYCLE WHEEL,
PRAM WHEEL ETC.

"Single action – Needle controlled" airbrushes are a minority manufacture, despite which they are probably available in greater numbers in modellers' workshops than any other type. The reason for this is largely historic, for the Badger 200 (the most widely used modelling airbrush internationally) was the first device to be widely marketed expressly for modellers, and it was many years before the hobby woke up to the availability of other styles. The single action airbrush, as its name suggests, has a control knob that only moves one way – up and down. This controls the air flow as before, but not the paint. Paint flow is still controlled by a tapered needle, but it is *not* a function of its design to move this needle during use. Instead its position within the paint jet is preset with a rear mounted screw before painting commences. This, of course, removes the finesse associated with double action airbrushes, for one can no longer vary the width and depth of the spray pattern *while the device is in use*. This does not, however, make it any the less useful for many applications and its continued wide sales support this point.

The third major group is generally known as "needle-less". This is to say it does not have the finely tapered control needle associated with the previous two styles. It does have a sort of needle, which once more is a pre-settable device, but the principle of operation is somewhat different with this design of airbrush in that the air and paint nozzles are no longer concentric but are external to the body of the airbrush and inclined at an angle to each other. The principle here is that air expelled from the air jet passes over the top of the paint jet and syphons off paint as it goes. Generally speaking these airbrushes exhibit less finesse, will not produce such fine lines and are perhaps better used for all-over colouring. Despite this, care, born out of practice, can still produce devastating effects.

Right at the bottom end of the range of spraying devices is the mini-spray gun (often still referred to as an airbrush for modelling). This takes the design of the needle-less gun to its ultimate simplicity and the end result is not very different from Edwardian and Victorian scent sprays.

As with paint-brushes, airbrushes are a "horses for courses" subject and to cover all aspects of spray painting properly one may well need more than one airbrush, as one would need more than one size of paint brush.

For larger models, the light industrial spray gun of the type used to touch up automobiles is by far the best bet. At this point it might be as well to pose the question, where do we get all this fancy gear? It is probably fair to assume that many of the specialised items used by

Small compressor units may use either a pump or a diaphragm system. For airbrush or small spray gun use, graphic art suppliers are often a useful source of small units and much other equipment.

the artist will need to be sought out from specialist art shops. Similarly spray guns and like equipment will need to be obtained from the factors that supply the motor touch-up and repair dealers. Most towns will have both art stores and motor supply factors and a quick scan through the yellow pages will yield their whereabouts.

Reverting to the spray gun scene, here we see a much bigger tool than the airbrush but obeying much the same principle, embodying tapered needle, concentric air and paint nozzles and a "double action" type of control which in this instance is initiated by the single action of a trigger, most often mounted beneath the body pistol-fashion. Paint pots of from a couple of ounces up to one and a half pints are commonplace and coverage will vary from a scant 1/16in. to up to 6in. wide.

Of course the use of all spraying devices of this nature relies on a source of compressed air and this is, more often than not, the stumbling block when selecting the right equipment for the job. For small airbrushes and intermittent use, the aerosol of pressurised freon is quite suitable. It *does* have restrictions but they can be mastered with a little practice. Larger airbrushes and spraying equipment demand a great deal more air (as does quantity use of the smaller airbrushes) and to this end there is little real choice but to use a compressor. Once more we are faced with an enormous choice of products over a very wide financial base. Many would-be users of spray equipment have come seriously unstuck over the choice of the right type of compressor to such an extent that in some cases airbrushing has become a rude word. It is *essential* that some expert advice is obtained before making what may amount to a significant investment, to ensure that the airbrush and compressor are not only compatible with each other but compatible with the type and size of model that one intends painting.

Perhaps more so than with brush painting, spraying requires much practice, but the rewards are worthwhile and, as with the selection of paint-brushes, it pays to invest in the better quality products within the range that best suits your particular sphere of modelling. The more able modeller will be easily and quickly aware of cost savings in the manufacture of home-made compressors (also detailed in the previous book) and will be more than aware of the safety factors to be observed.

In use, spraying equipment fills the surrounding air with atomised paint (not just the fumes as with a paint-brush) and this can pose several problems. The health hazard is now much higher, for one tends to breath in paint particles rather than solvent vapour and adequate safety precautions are to be considered (see later). Furthermore one must consider the nature of these paint particles. Rapid drying paints such as cellulose and matt enamels will tend to dry while suspended in the air and will land dry, forming an unpleasant layer of dust. This dust may easily be removed with a soft cloth. Slower drying paints, gloss enamels, epoxies, polyesters etc., will land whilst still wet and *dry where they land*. The tenacious nature of modern paints makes them extremely difficult to remove once dry – so be warned – *DON'T* spray paints in areas where this could be a problem. White paint fall-out on, say, a pristine black night-fighter model is at the very least a nuisance. So is the problem of removing epoxy overspray off the dining room suite!

Like paint-brushes, airbrushes and spray guns must be stored properly and kept scrupulously clean. Different manufacturers recommend different cleaning techniques, but whichever method is chosen remember that "cleanliness is next to Godliness"! Look after your spray equipment and it will serve you faithfully for a lifetime.

Aerosols

There are of course other routes to successful painting and while we are still on the subject of spraying one should not lightly dismiss the aerosol can. Paint pre-packaged in this manner is largely limited to D.I.Y. oil-bound paints of, largely, the common gloss colours, or cellulose-based paints for the touching up of the odd scratch on a car. A wide choice of colours is available from this latter source, and in some cases these can be a reasonable shade match to some of the camouflage colours. However, a couple of problems do emerge. The large areas of cover necessitate using some form of stencil or masking when painting smaller models, which works but is wasteful of paint. The other snag is the lack of specific shades to match certain model colours.

The alternative here is to utilise one of the "refillable" aerosols which may be pumped up with either a bicycle pump or a motor car foot pump. This now offers the modeller the ability to put his own paint into the can, pump it up and spray. Again one is restricted to reasonably large areas of cover, reasonable large volumes of paint (it will consume lots of ½oz. jars!) and the relatively short bursts of use between pumping up. For most modelling purposes this is not too much of a problem since the areas are usually fairly small, which means that they can be sprayed at one application.

Another spray item never used for modelling yet well worth using is a graphics product known as "Letrajet" and marketed by the Letraset company. This is a unique gadget that can be driven from an aerosol or from a compressor and uses, would you believe, a felt tip pen for its source of colour. "Pantone" is another Letraset branded system of

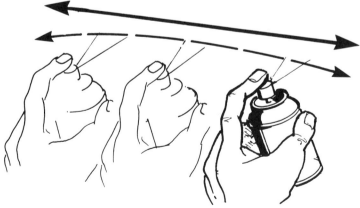

KEEP SPRAY CAN PARALLEL TO WORK AT ALL TIMES -
DO NOT USE CURVED WRIST ACTION

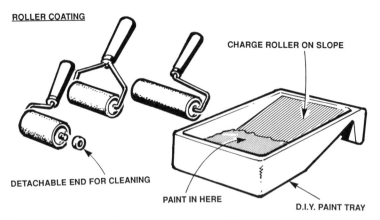

ROLLER COATING

CHARGE ROLLER ON SLOPE

DETACHABLE END FOR CLEANING

PAINT IN HERE

D.I.Y. PAINT TRAY

SHEEPSKIN ROLLER COVERS ARE BEST FOR EMULSION PAINTS,
(CLEAN IN WATER). FOR APPLYING RESINS (POLYESTER AND EPOXY)
AND FOR WING SKINNING ETC.   USE DISPOSABLE SPONGE COVERS

standardised, matching colours widely adopted by the graphic arts
business. Pantone felt tip pens come in a choice of several hundred
colour-keyed shades that many art people use as "standards". These
felt pens fit into the handle of the Letrajet airbrush and the action of the
expelled air, behaving very much like the needle-less airbrush, literally siphons the ink from the tip of the pen as it passes by.

Tradition has made us all conscious of "paint" as a finishing
medium for models, but as was seen in Chapter 1, there is a definitive
area where felt tips, inks and watercolours can be satisfactorily used
in model making. If one of these avenues is yours, then the Letrajet
system will open up the felt tip pen approach to include the infinite
shaded edge more usually associated with spraying or airbrushing.

Rollers

From the sophisticated to the ridiculous, the miniature versions of the
D.I.Y. paint rollers (usually only found in good quality art shops or
made from scrap by the more enthusiastic amongst us) have a
specific part to play in model finishing. Later in this book the subject of
"pre-finish techniques" is discussed fully and mention has already
been made of polyester resin which may well be used for this purpose.
Resin-coating wings of large model aircraft can be both time-consuming and uneven if done by brush, and there is little to gain by thinning
the resin to spraying consistency. The short "pot life" or working time
allowable with resins of this nature requires a rapid and even coating
and roller coating is a good way to achieve these results on such large
and virtually flat areas.

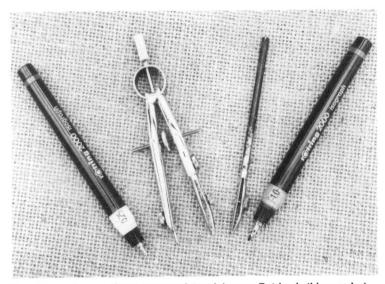

Draughtsman's pens. Outer are proprietary ink pens, Rotring in this case but there are many others. Number on coloured ring on barrel indicates the width of drawn line in mm. Central is older style bow pen, both hand-held and mounted in compasses.

Pens

Of course, no discussion on "tools of the trade" would be complete without mentioning the ancillary items, many of which are commonplace.

Lining pens are useful for all manner of fine line work and have a particular place in lining out locomotives and for fine line work on military figures. Most lining pens are of the "split nib" type where the gap between the nibs is adjustable to define the line width. Most inks, water colours and thin paints can be used in this type of pen but rapid-drying paints may well give trouble by drying out within the nib and causing flow blockage. These pens are "loaded" with colour from a brush or a bulb and glass "dropper" and should not be dipped into the fluid. The paint should only be *between* the nibs, NEVER on the outside edge.

An extension to this type of lining pen is the dual system with two pairs of nibs, useful for drawing two lines parallel but not necessarily of the same width. Invaluable for locomotive and traction engine lining!

Yet another extension of the use of this type of pen is that they can be obtained to fit into the end of a pair of draughtsman's compasses and thereby provide perfectly drawn circles. No more the ragged roundel on that super camouflaged Spitfire or Lancaster?

DRAUGHTSMAN'S BOW PEN

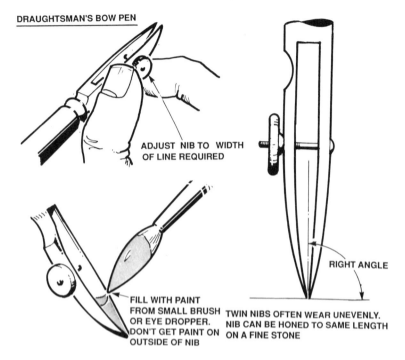

ADJUST NIB TO WIDTH
OF LINE REQUIRED

RIGHT ANGLE

FILL WITH PAINT
FROM SMALL BRUSH   TWIN NIBS OFTEN WEAR UNEVENLY.
OR EYE DROPPER.   NIB CAN BE HONED TO SAME LENGTH
DON'T GET PAINT ON ON A FINE STONE
OUTSIDE OF NIB

In fact a decent set of draughtsman's tools will make a valuable contribution to any modeller's tool kit. Compasses are an essential element of any form of circular painting and in future chapters they, and the accessories to fit them, will come more to the fore. Additional fine line devices of immense use are the fountain type draughtsman's pens. Virtually all of the famous names in draughting produce pens of

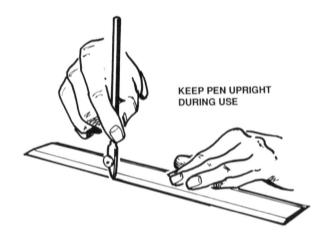

KEEP PEN UPRIGHT
DURING USE

this "stylus nib" style, whose action is to provide the draughtsman with an ink line of constant width. Standard line thicknesses vary from 0.18mm to 2.0mm and pens may be bought singly or in sets. Many sets of compasses have adaptors to enable these pens to be used in place of the bow nib pen.

For the majority of draughting work, these pens are filled with black indian ink (ideal for panel lines) but they can be used with virtually any of the current crop of artists' inks, offering the end user a wide choice of colour. More recently the drawing office world has seen a flood of new kinds of pens and pencils into its already overcrowded market. Just one such range is the fibre tipped pen which is directly compatible with standard draughting pens (that is to say they produce constant width lines of matching widths to existing pens). There is no room in this type of pen to change colours, but the basic colours are usually available and while one cannot necessarily buy these pens to match, say, G.W.R. lining colours, the black pen can be a very low cost investment for production of panel lines in quite small scales as well as fine detail work on military figures.

3 SURFACE PREPARATION

As the old adage goes – beauty is only skin deep! No amount of surface paint will disguise bad workmanship. Furthermore, it might be argued that with modern spray and airbrush techniques, for example, colour is deposited upon a surface thinner and more evenly than any previous painting method. This factor could well be of immense importance to, say, the plastic kit enthusiast, for as we have seen over the years, the development of the toolmaker's art has produced such fineness in terms of panel detail that even one heavy-handed brush coat can all but eliminate it.

On the other hand, models of mixed material construction could well come to rely on heavy coats of primer or undercoat to assist in building up an even surface prior to painting.

So, if painting a model is important, preparation for painting is even more so!

Surface preparation techniques would fill a book all on their own. Many different approaches are valid for many different materials and subjects. A brief chapter such as this can only hope to touch on some of the more popular techniques. Let us first consider the flying model. Today's model aircraft vary structurally and in size and performance from the minuscule "Peanut scale" free flight models spanning a scant 13 inches to the radio-controlled giants of 10-15 feet wing span, with correspondingly huge variations in weight.

Primers and Fillers

For the smaller models, weight is without doubt the prime consideration, and it is unlikely that anything other than an airbrush will be used for the surface colouring. Very light structures such as this will almost certainly be tissue covered over a balsa frame and little real pre-finish will be needed or indeed can be accepted on the grounds of weight. Larger models are a different kettle of fish and here pre-finish becomes of greater consequence. Balsa wood is still the prime structural medium and the need to paint over balsa is and has been a major stumbling block for many a long year. The grain of balsa is particularly

"Superfiller" by London's Aero Model Mart is an excellent example of modern products. Basically it is a micro-balloon product carried in a water-based emulsion. Adheres well to most surfaces and sands to a lightweight, supersmooth finish.

Rubbing down can be an area of concern too, for to attack the surface with glasspaper can vary from the moderate success to the absolute disaster. Far better, if one has to rub down dry, is to use garnet paper. Garnet paper is the brick red coloured stuff which in general produces a better finish and does not clog so easily. For the really best results, however, the use of wet or dry paper is to be recommended. Wet or dry may be used dry, as its names suggests, or wet, which is to be preferred in most cases. Lubrication with warm soapy water enables a much better cut to be obtained, resulting in a smoother surface, with less effort and far less clogging of the paper.

Another area in aeromodelling where the grain of wood is a problem is the modern trend toward foam wings. Here wings are pre-cut out from expanded polystyrene foam and covered with wood. Most British manufacturers use obechi veneer although some of our Continental cousins (and those from the U.S.A.) use balsa wood.

Obechi is an open grain wood and will require similar treatment to that of balsa. Where extra care is needed in treating foam wings is the fact that clear dopes and sanding sealers dissolve the foam rapidly and immediately on contact. Consequently it is important during the structural phase of the wing assembly to ensure that all joints are secure and that there are no splits in the grain. Without this additional care and attention dope or sanding sealer will without doubt find its way inside, destroying the wing. Apart from this, the same procedure can be adopted as with sheeted balsa surfaces.

Of course a "tissue over wood" finish presupposes that the basic surface and shape were right to start with and to this end several proprietary products can be brought to bear. Interior grade Polyfilla may be used to fill minor dents or blemishes prior to tissue covering. However, it will pay to go easy, for fillers of this type are heavy and add nothing to the structural integrity of the model. Building up "special" bumps and blisters, fairings and trimmings can often be done with balsa, grain filling as you go, but the use of primer fillers, stoppers and G.R.P. fillers can often be of immense assistance. Stoppers and high build primers are nearly always of cellulose base, although some of the modern fillers and primers are of the two-pack synthetic variety.

Filler/primers are widely used in the motor car repair world and should be available from the specialist car repair dealers. They can be bought in cans suitable for brushing (or, heavily thinned, spraying) or in convenient aerosols. Colour varies from brand to brand but will usually be a flat neutral grey. The pigment in these primers builds extra thickness rapidly and therefore several coats will cover up most blemishes, though adding weight in the process. Stoppers, on the other hand, are similar in formulation but much more heavily pigmented to produce a consistency of very thick treacle (or even thicker). These products tend to be applied with a flat palette type of knife blade into particularly bad blemishes. Both stoppers and primer/fillers tend to dry largely by evaporation and it is therefore better to apply several coats, allowing adequate time to dry right through between coats, rather than to try to build up the surface all in one go. Heavy coats of stopper will tend to contract and sink during drying and if the surface has been flattened off before the "insides" have fully hardened, then the resulting "dip" will be less than acceptable.

Modern plastic fillers are two-part devices of the polyester family. Many are produced expressly for the motor "patch up" brigade and can be used for modelling with equal success. Many of them are heavy and require to be used in moderation, and most of them contain

Artists' palette knives are excellent for applying stopper pastes and the like, as well as their primary use of mixing oil colours.

solvents that may attack polystyrene – so keep them away from foam wing cores. Most of these fillers are in paste form and can be roughly moulded to shape with the fingers or with home made spatulas whilst still in the uncured state. Cellulose thinner or water may be used as a lubricant for this shaping exercise. Once dry they can be sawn, filed, drilled and sanded to virtually any shape that is required. Specialist epoxy putties can also be used in this way but, again, while of immense strength, they are not exactly light in weight. For large-area filling, such as producing wing fillets for instance, much lighter fillers are needed and one should shop around for such specialist light-weight products as one can find. SIG Epoxolite is a lightweight epoxy putty much favoured. Other brands of polyester filling paste have particularly low specific gravity and some are so light they they float on water – buoyancy aids for model boats perhaps.

Low weight fillers of this nature are a better bet for large area filling although they do not exhibit the same high strength and in some cases might benefit from a balsa or ply former on which to build.

From time to time the need arises for a specifically high strength filler, perhaps in an area where a fastening is required. Aluminium loaded epoxies fill this bill without massive weight increases. This type of filler is strong enough to be machined and can be drilled and tapped for fixing screws.

One other type of filler worthy of a passing mention is the body fillers used for plastic kits. Covered later in this chapter, these fillers can be useful for small detail work on flying models.

An alternative for pre-finishing wood surfaces has come as a by-product of the glass fibre resin age. Most polyester resins used for structural parts in modelling and many other amateur or basic mould-ing applications tend to cure leaving a sticky layer on the surface. Most of this is due to the fact that damp air acts as an inhibitor and stops the cure taking place. As only the top surface is in contact with the atmosphere, the remainder of the cure takes place without bother.

Sanding the cured resin is messy, for this sticky outer surface picks up in the garnet or glass paper and rapidly clogs, but washing with methylated spirit or acetone will remove the top layer and allow better attention with the sanding block. To avoid the problem altogether there have been developed resins marketed expressly as "finishing" or "preparation" resins. These are to all intents and purposes the same to apply as a structural resin, except that by way of complex chemical formula adaptation they cure completely dry. There is a layer of very fine wax upon the cured surface which has no effect on the sanding process but *will* cause problems with subsequent paint

Dope, tissue and sanding sealer are giving way to modern resins as a prefinish medium. Two American market leaders, K & B Super Poxy and Hobbypoxy, both market preparation resins. Despite the company brand names both prefinishes are POLYESTER resins and must not be used on foams and plastics.

adhesion. Therefore paint should not be applied directly onto cured resins – only onto a sanded resin surface.

Finishing wood and veneer with these resins is very quick and simple and removes any need for dope, sealers or tissue. Simply brush or roller the activated resin directly onto the wood, spread well out and allow to cure. Curing time, like any other two-part resin, is dependent upon temperature, but at an ambient of 70°F, cure is usually effected within an hour or two or overnight if working in winter weather.

Subsequent investigation of the result might well prove frightening, for the grain of wood will have been raised and the whole surface will have dried out looking like coarse glasspaper. Don't despair – it's meant to be like this! Don't try to sand it smooth but, using reasonably coarse garnet, say 80 grit, rub over the surface to remove the worst of the sharp peaks, dust off and apply a second coat. When this second coat has cured, attack the whole surface with progressively finer grades of garnet paper starting with 120 grit and finishing with as fine a grade as you feel necessary.

For most models this is all that is needed, although for really bad areas a third coat, or partial coat, may be required. Major dents and dings may be filled with Polyfilla prior to applying resin, or can actually be filled with resin mixed with a powder. The most advanced techniques call for advanced materials and the best filler to use with resins is micro balloons. These have the appearance of fine face pow-

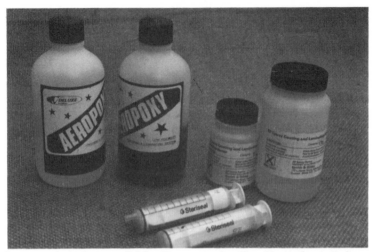

Some people prefer to pre-finish with epoxy resins; if working on foam you have no choice! Shown are two such resins, Aeropoxy and Smith & Gibbs SP113, which are widely used in the U.K. Unlike polyester finishing resins, greater time is needed to effect a full cure and several days is usual before rubbing down.

der but in point of fact are tiny hollow glass balls. They weigh next to nothing and can be sanded to a fine surface finish. Consequently they can be added to resins to provide the "bulk" without the added weight.

Great strength is added to balsa and veneer by virtue of the resin soaking into the surface, but like dopes and sanding sealers, polyester finishing resins attack foam, so one should ensure that there is no passage for the resin to enter a veneered surface.

For even greater strength balsa or veneered surfaces can be covered with fabric such as nylon using resin as an adhesive. Still further steps can be made by covering the surface with lightweight glass cloth or even the incorporation of such "miracle" products as carbon fibre, Boron or Kevlar fibres. Building these materials into the resin layer can add overall or localised strength as part of the pre-finishing process.

Resins of this nature (polyester or epoxy) produce a surface finish virtually identical to that of factory made glass-fibre fuselages and perhaps this is the time to consider those.

Glass Fibre Components

Most G.R.P. fuselages, boat hulls etc. are made from polyester resins and glass cloths although some higher priced, high quality overseas products are made using epoxy resins. From the finishing point of view there is little difference. The prime concern is that of adhesion, for epoxy resins do not stick too well to polyesters and vice-versa. This manifests itself when sticking other parts to the mouldings more than in the finishing phase.

Most moulded glass products will feature pigmented resins and therefore are self-coloured right through from the outer gloss surface coat to the inner face. Theoretically this only leaves fine detail painting to be done to the outer face. In practice, however, joints in G.R.P. mouldings are rarely perfect and some degree of filling and rubbing down will be needed to blend these joints in perfectly. Whichever way one tackles this, it is likely to show, and then the only real answer is to paint it all over. The biggest problem in painting G.R.P. mouldings lies in the fact that the surface will almost certainly feature traces of wax or silicone release agent used to stop the resinous gel coat from sticking to the mould during the moulding process. This will cause severe adhesion problems for paints and primers, and *MUST* be removed. Washing in solvent or in strong solutions of hot soapy water will get rid of most of it, but far and away the best course is to wet-and-dry the whole of the outside surface to provide a key for subsequent paint coats. During this pnase any necessary filling can be achieved using the appropriate resin and micro balloons. Subsequent rubbing down will produce a smooth level surface that will take primers, fillers etc. without problem. At this stage one can now give the entire model a coat of primer. Ordinary cellulose primer is adequate and readily available from most motor factors, although if it is intended to work right through with epoxide paints, for example, then it might well be of benefit to start with the matching epoxy primer.

The main use for a primer is the production of an overall flat finish which will form a bond between the bare material and the colour coats. Its major by-product is to show up every blemish in the structure beneath and this is the point at which to consider whether you've achieved sufficient of a standard. A really good preparation will be revealed by lightly wet 'n drying the primer right off! Of course this then removes the ability to see the surface provided by the primer. A good tip here, then, is to use two different brands of primer of different colours, say light grey and dark grey. When you consider that your surface finish is satisfactory, lightly spray on a coat of contrasting colour primer and allow to dry. Now cut it back with fine grade wet 'n dry paper, used wet. If your initial surface was flat, the whole of this contrasting colour primer will vanish. If it does not but stays around in patches then the original surface was not as flat as you thought it was, for the patches of colour will show up the "low lying" areas and further work will be required.

All foam or foam/balsa structures cannot be pre-finished with cellulose or polyester resins. Epoxy resin used here with surface defects filled with Aero Model Mart waterbased microballoon filler. Adequate subsequent sanding is essential to create a perfect surface for colour coats.

Mixed material models are always difficult to pre-finish, e.g. with plastic cowls on a balsa/ply fuselage, any pre-finish (resins, primers etc.) must be compatible with *all* the materials. Here the plastic parts are A.B.S. and therefore cellulose primer can be used. Always try out the pre-finish on scrap material first.

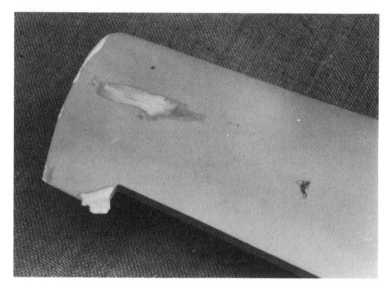

"Hangar Rash", i.e. damage due to handling during finishing. Major damage can be cured by using a mixture of microballoons with resin, PVA, epoxy or whatever medium is compatible with the original surface. Dent in wing and tip damage built up in this way prior to final sanding.

Mixed finish routes. G.R.P. fuselage usually requires gentle attention with wet or dry or steel wool to remove surface grease and/or join lines. Tail plane is balsa and finishing resin. Elevators are tissue and dope over balsa and then grey primer sanded back. Rudder is bare balsa yet to be finished.

Metals

Far less pre-finishing is needed with metal models, for, in general, the surface of the metal itself will be grain-free and unless scarred or mal-treated is likely to have a good enough finish. Of course where there *are* blemishes, the fillers, stoppers and resin based pastes used for car body work are still valid. Conventional primers can be used on metal models but it is worth considering just what metals are in use. Brass, copper, nickel-silver and various steels are widely used in rail-way models from the smaller OO gauges up to the larger live steam models. The main problem with these types of metals is that they oxidise amazingly quickly. So quickly in fact that even if one was to polish down to the base metal, oxides would form on the surface be-fore one could have a chance to apply any paint! Oxides of this nature are death to painting for they reject any adhesion from the majority of paints and primers. The answer to this is a special kind of primer con-taining an active acid. The acid eats through the oxide layer and actu-ally attacks the bare metal. This attack is quite ferocious, but microscopic, so that you won't see the model disappear in front of your eyes! The microscopic attack, though, artificially roughens the surface and provides a key for the primer to adhere to. From here on in, paints and normal primers will adhere to the etch primer.

In general etch primers are of low viscosity (i.e. they are somewhat runny) and maybe of single or two-pack form. Because of the acid content, they are most usually packaged in jars or plastic bottles rather than cans. Two-pack etch primers will often have the base resin in a can with the acid hardener in a jar. Many modellers fight shy of etch primers because the thought of the acid content scares them off.

Single and two-pack etch primers don't work in quite the same way. Single pack products are usually of the "dry etch" family wherein the etching process doesn't actually start until the primer is dry. Two-packs etch *all of the time* once the two parts are mixed together. The obvious conclusion to be drawn from here is that one must be careful when applying two-part etchants to immediately and scrupulously clean out the equipment used. It is not difficult to imagine the horror in people's minds at the thought of the insides of an expensive airbrush being eaten away by acid! In point of fact this would only happen if the spray head and needle were not thoroughly cleaned immediately that the primering was complete.

Etch primers are, in general, only required in the thinnest possible layer commensurate with covering the subject all over. They do not, by and large, build up the surface like primer/fillers or high build prim-ers, although there are some products that contradict this and these will be discussed later. Many etchants are clear, like water, and though they should be applied as thinly as possible, their transparency makes it difficult to see where you've been and the tendency is to keep on applying more. This does absolutely nothing for the quality of the etch or that of the surface finish. In fact it could have an adverse effect, for multiple wet coats will often cause problems where the surface coat dries first causing "solvent entrapment" beneath. As the solvents in the undercoatings can no longer evaporate, the lower coats stay wet and sticky for a very long time. Remember that etching primers need only to cover entirely. Subsequent coats can be made with conventional primers.

This problem of solvent entrapment is common to all aspects of multiple paint coats and should be borne in mind at every stage of the game, not just the pre-finishing stages. Another problem with etch primer is that they use a special thinner. This thinner should *not* be used with any other paint or primer and other thinners will *not* work with etch primers. If no special thinner is required, then one can be fairly certain that the primer in question is not an etchant. Using the wrong thinner with etch primers will almost certainly make the primer unusable, probably causing settling out of pigment (like fine sand in the bottom of the jar) or thickening to the consistency of glue, either of which means a dustbin situation.

Etch primers can be brushed or sprayed but many of them have a strong odour and reasonable safety precautions need to be observed.

Plastics

Apart from wood, glass fibre and metal, the biggest area of model painting is almost certainly the ubiquitous "Airfix" kit. Plastic modelling has grown from simple beginnings that were frowned upon by traditionalists to a major following in its own right. The serious student of this form of modelling will not take no for an answer to any of his problems, particularly that of colour rendition. The fit of parts of the modern plastic kit is exemplary and, properly assembled, no real filling or priming should be necessary, only a wipe over with hot soapy water to remove any traces of mould release agent before starting to paint. Problems really only begin with the wish to modify, convert, change or generally adapt one kit into another, a process which finishes with the modeller working from scratch.

In these circumstances models that start off as all-plastic often wind up being of mixed material construction. Here one has a myriad of problems which all culminate in the desire for a "common" surface finish prior to painting. Special fillers are available for the plastic en-

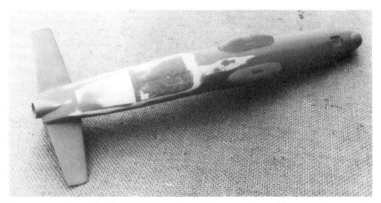

Part-prepared plastic kit. Model has already been coated with grey primer and rubbed down to reveal the blemishes. Squadron products "Green Stuff" putty has been applied to fill the stand hole and make good the poor fit of the rear loading doors. When the putty has been rubbed smooth with wet or dry paper, the whole model will be re-primered.

thusiast and these are obtainable from the specialist suppliers to the hobby. These fillers can be used for plugging up badly fitting parts, modelling non-provided parts or for surfacing major alterations. Where major alterations are carried out in wood, they may be surfaced with thin layers of body filler, or may revert to the dope, sanding sealer, tissue or resin treatment discussed earlier. Take care, however, on mixed material models, for as we have seen some resins, fillers and sealers attack polystyrene.

While in general it is fair to say that styrene models should never be painted with cellulose or even some acrylics, later chapters will show how some techniques will overcome the problem. The same applies to moulded plastic parts for model aircraft and boats: application of dopes to such parts, particularly if applied thickly with a brush, will almost certainly cause them to melt into a useless mess.

As we have seen several times before, our saviour often comes from someone else's industry. In this case one needs to look again towards the motor refinishing industry. It will come as no surprise to the uninitiated to learn that this industry is vast – bigger in fact than the motor manufacturing industry – for far more people "bend" cars than buy new ones.

Mixed Materials

Modern day motor cars feature many plastic parts and a respray will involve painting the metal parts and the plastic parts in situ. This requirement has led to the need of the paint manufacturers to develop "special" etch primers that will equally attack the plastic and the metal. Regrettably we are back to the problem of quantity, for it is not possible to buy these products in ½oz. tinlets or jars, but as primer is a universal product that will be used on *all* models whereas specific paint colours will pertain only to specific models, buying primer by the litre is perhaps less of a hardship. Some of these special primers are also high-build items capable of multiple coatings that can obliterate surface detail. They all require their own special thinner. This type of product is a good universal primer, for it can be lightly sprayed onto a quality plastic kit but laid more heavily, in multiple coats, over wooden and other "adaptations", blending in to provide that elusive result, the same common overall finish.

One area of plastic not covered here is moulded expanded polystyrene. This is not overly widespread in modelling but its uses are not confined only to cores for flying models. Cut with a hot wire it can be pressed into service as scenery for model railway layouts, cut into sheet for children's forts and dolls' houses and made into letters to decorate model club stands at local displays and exhibitions.

As we have seen earlier, most solvents attack expanded foam, leaving a sticky mess. Oil and water-based products are probably the only "safe" materials to use. For display and scenic work, household emulsion paint (a water-based synthetic resin) is more than adequate applied by brush or roller. For flying models with exposed foam surfaces proprietary oil-bound or water-based paints will do but please go easy on their application, for the open nature of this type of plastic can consume paint and add weight at an alarming rate.

4 HANDLING PAINTS

There is much that one ought to know about handling paints before letting fly with some onto your latest modelling products.

Paint, in general, should not be used straight from the tin.

Paint, in general, will separate out with the pigment sinking to the bottom of the can.

Paint, in general, is never the right consistency.

Need I go on?

Paint should be stored properly. Cold and frost can affect paint, therefore it is best stored indoors rather than out in the garden shed. I had a disaster when a gallon can of a particularly difficult-to-match colour rusted through on the floor of the shed. I'd gone to some lengths, some twenty years ago, to obtain the *exact* shade, mixed specially by one of the country's largest manufacturers, in the knowledge that a gallon would last me all my modelling life. Imagine then my language when almost all of the remaining four pints or so spread evenly across the shed floor and dried there when the can simply rusted through! If you can do it, store paints in a reasonable environment – loft, cellar, cupboard under the stairs or anywhere where they won't freeze.

The major factor in all painting is to make absolutely sure that the pigment is *totally* in suspension prior to and during use. Regrettably, 90% of modellers pay only cursory lip service to this problem. A quick shake or a superficial stir with an offcut of sprue is all that it gets. Perfectly mixed paint is that where each granule of pigment is totally surrounded by the carrying medium and is not attached to any other grain – a tall order.

Unfortunately much falls by the wayside when this result is not achieved. Adhesion suffers, colour match deteriorates and the degree of "gloss" or "flat" may change. Furthermore, where modern, chemically-produced paints (rather than the older "natural" varieties) are in use, the exact chemical reaction may be affected to the extent that some of the specific properties associated with the paints may be reduced or even disappear completely.

Hand stirring is best done with a broad flat stick rather than a round wire or screwdriver.

Of course the whole subject of colour matching could fill a book on its own, and there would be many who would deny the experts on the grounds that the prototype would, more than likely, have been painted from a 5-gallon container that had been only cursorily stirred! How many Spitfires or Messerschmitts, for instance, were repainted "in the field" with less than adequate attention to what was being done? However, we will return to this later.

The golden rule with mixing of proprietary paints is that one can never stir too much. Only a really thorough exercise here will yield the result for which the manufacturer has expended much time and energy. Not only do we need to separate the lumps of congealed pigments but where "flatting" or "dulling" agents are used, these should be dispersed evenly throughout a homogeneous mixture.

The instruments needed and the time taken are the key to success. For hand mixing, do not use a round section rod. Due to the good aerodynamic shape of a round object the paint will part each side of the rod and not be disturbed sufficiently to achieve satisfactory results. A flat spatula shape is usually better and a clean flat stick is preferable to a screwdriver, which is made to turn screws.

Stirring Although paint left to stand settles out, causing this need for stirring, there is some advantage in leaving freshly stirred paint standing for, say, half an hour or so before returning to start stirring again. Often this short standing period will reveal that the paint wasn't truly in suspension when you left off. Properly stirred paint is unlikely to settle in such a short space of time while poorly stirred paint almost certainly will. There are a couple of useful ideas from the full-size

Stirrer from coathanger wire in 12V mini drill. Paint tinlet held firm in vice secured to drill stand.

brigade that bear passing on for they work well for the modeller. One consists of power stirring and the other power shaking. Powered stirring is not as unusual as it might seem. The prime requirement is a wire stirrer which can be made from thin steel wire; about 18 SWG piano wire is suitable for smaller tinlets but heavy duty coat-hanger wire is better for cans of 1/4 pint or more. While the exact shape and size of the stirrer are unimportant, the wire should be roughly "Z" shaped with the height of the Z equal to about two-thirds of the can height and the width of the Z as big as possible commensurate with entry through the lid of the can.

Now a circular section was seen to be incorrect for hand stirring, so why then does it work here? Well, the answer is the speed at which we aim to rotate this wire stirrer. Hand stirring breaks up the paint by direct contact, but power stirring uses the "vortex" or "whirlpool" effect caused by the rapid movement of the stirrer. Of course having made a stirrer, it then has to be turned at some sensible speed while ensuring that the can doesn't move as well. The ideal stirrer is a motor-driven bench drill. Many of today's modellers will have already discovered the advantages of small precision model drills from such famous names as Precision Petite, Como and Black and Decker's Minicraft range. Most of these tools are 12 volt D.C. operated and can rev up to 10-20,000 rpm. Using the universal power supplies now common to these tool ranges, a rotational speed of around 3-4,000 rpm will produce excellent stirring in quite short times. Because of this relatively high speed, it is essential that the can is held rigidly and accurately in place relative to the axis of the drill and stirrer. This can be done by hand, for most gloss colours will mix effectively in about two minutes or so and matt colours just a little longer. However, a far better practice is to use a vertical drill stand to keep the drill and stirrer upright and at the correct height while retaining the can in a universal vice that can be screwed or clamped to the base of the stand. Such alignment and retention not only guarantee success but free the operator for other tasks. If a variable speed controller is used then it pays to switch on at low speed and increase it to about the right stirring speed, rather than switching on at stirring speed. This then tends to reduce any initial splashing.

Power shaking takes a great deal longer but can be carried out remotely, say overnight, as it does not require that the operator remains in attendance. I've seen two different ways of doing it and both seem to work alright. The first used a domestic orbital sander, although the Black and Decker Minicraft unit would probably do just as well. A large lump of Blu-tak was used to hold the can in place upon the sole plate and the sander fitted upside down in the vice.

The other trick used an old 10in. loudspeaker with the moving coil supporting a thin Formica plate to which the paint tin was clamped using a couple of grooved hardwood blocks. Running the speaker coil at 50 c.p.s. from a suitable step down transformer (6 volts appears to be more than adequate) produced sufficient vibration.

Dropping three or four bearing balls into the paint pot and replacing the lid tightly would also seem to be a good move.

Some enthusiasts will not work from anything other than a pristine tin of paint. Others, by dint of sound economics or by way of having to mix special shades, *need* to store mixed colours and to this end many would advise storing jars or cans upside down to effect a better seal. This is a doubtful practice, for any damage is likely to be caused by the air trapped in the tin, whether it be at the top or the bottom.

Opening old tins of paint may well reveal a set skin that should be carefully removed. If bits drop into the paint then straining (or filtering) through the finest mesh old stocking will help to remove the pieces. Jars with screw lids may well jam up when stored and a useful trick to loosen them involves standing the jar upside down in a heat-proof saucer and pouring very hot water into the saucer up to the level of the cap only (don't let the water come into contact with the glass). The resulting temperature rise will cause the cap to expand and the lid will easily unscrew – take care not to burn your fingers!

There is no point in mixing paint up thoroughly unless its consistency is right to start with and a greater or lesser amount of thinner is usually needed to obtain the correct results. Many would counsel that paint should not be stored ready thinned but should be decanted into small containers and thinned for use, the remainder being firmly re-capped and stored. Most paints *can* be brushed "straight from the can" but most will benefit from about 10%-20% addition of thinners. For spraying applications as much as 70% thinner may need adding, dependent upon the original consistency of the paint. (Some automobile paints are like treacle!) The best spraying consistency is determined by using "viscosity cups" where a measured volume is allowed to flow through a given size outlet hole. Correct viscosity is achieved when the flow breaks into droplets after an exact measured time. This type of measurement is rarely used in the amateur world and the general rule of thumb is to aim for the consistency of creamy milk. Too thick and the paint will obscure surface detail and dry "knob-bly" like the skin of an orange. Too thin and the paint won't cover first time round. DO NOT be tempted to put more on, it will only run!! Rather let the first coat dry and add more, single coats until the build-up is sufficient.

Remember, whether brushing or spraying, the old adage "many light coats are better than one heavy coat" still holds good today.

Of course multiple coating brings with it its own crop of problems. *Always* allow each coat to dry thoroughly as, if not, the second coat could well dry first causing "solvent entrapment". That, as previously mentioned, is where the solvents of the first coat have nowhere to evaporate to due to the hard outer skin of the second coat. This can be an acute embarrassment, at best taking ages to dry and at worst – say if using cellulose on a plastic kit – causing the trapped solvents to soften and distort the plastic base.

Drying times vary from paint to paint and this also can be a cause of frustration. In general, matt paints dry faster, having more volatile sol-vents. Oil-bound paints of the "model enamel" type will be touch dry in a few minutes, as will matt cellulose and acrylics. Gloss enamels tend to have much longer drying times, presumably as these are gen-erally developed for brush application and the time is necessary to en-able the brush strokes to flow out. To be sure of adequate hardness, overnight drying is recommended. Special paints such as epoxides will have varying drying (curing) times dependent upon the hardener used. Brushing hardeners allow for the brush marks to flow out, as with enamels, and several hours is the norm. Spraying hardener sets up quicker and matt hardener quicker still – usually about an hour. Other specialist finishes, Tufkote for example, also cure sufficiently for handling in about an hour. Polyester finishing resins take about the same time and so do cellulose and acrylic primers.

Drying times quoted here can only act as a rough guide and are

An example of a modern balsa filler, Super Smoothcote is simply sprayed on (left) and sanded off (right). Two coats are usually enough for most models.

difficult to hide and considerable filling will be needed to obtain a perfectly smooth surface. Consider the production of an aircraft where the original's surface is of smooth metal, or perhaps worse, one of the newer plastic laminates. The pre-finish requirement is to remove all traces of wood grain and produce a smooth flat surface onto which to paint.

For years sanding sealer was considered the best grain filler. Sanding sealer is a cellulose based clear lacquer containing a powdery filler which when dry can be sanded smooth. Talcum powder mixed with clear dope is often put forward as a cheap alternative and this works almost as well. The action of these grain fillers is to coat the surface all over with the result that when rubbed down, the upper peaks of the wood are rubbed clear, leaving the filler in the troughs of the grain. Repeated application and rubbing down will eventually fill all of the troughs to a common and even level. This works in principle but in practice does tend to be hard work and grain lines can open up again when the top coats of colour are applied. A much better method is to lightly clear dope the structure all over, rub down lightly with medium grade garnet paper and then apply a layer of lightweight modelling tissue to the balsa, using a second coat of dope as an adhesive. Complex curves will need multiple pieces of tissue to negotiate them and it is best to tear the tissue rather than cut it. The soft torn edge will blend in with dope much more easily than hard cut edges. Now additional coats of thinned clear dope may be applied or one can revert to the use of sanding sealer. Several light coats, rubbing down between each coat, will result in a smooth, grain-free surface ready to paint.

based on "good" European temperatures – say about 20°C (68°F) and low relative humidity. Ambient conditions have a marked effect upon these times and one can, with caution, use ambients to control these times. Ready mixed two pack paints (epoxides for instance), can be stored in the domestic refrigerator – provided that they are well marked and not used by mistake in food preparation. Such storage will slow down the cure quite markedly and the paint may well stay usable for a number of days, maybe even a week or more (dependent upon brand and thickness). The reverse is also true. Warming the paint in a jar of hot water before application helps to make it more runny and cure more quickly. Use of a hot air gun (a hair dryer or Solarfilm shrinking gun) can also be used to speed up the drying time, but care should be exercised to avoid stirring up the dust in the atmosphere.

Not everybody recommends this route, but the "hot pot" heated paint spraying system has been standard in industry for many a long year and products such as Hobbypoxy actually recommend it!

Overcoating with the *same* brand and/or colour of paint is usually an accepted practice but even within accepted practices it is worth being careful. Matt enamels can quite easily soften when an overcoat is applied and where masking of upper and lower model colours is needed, the overbrushing can cause the lower colour to bleed into the

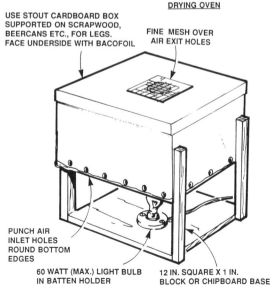

DRYING OVEN

USE STOUT CARDBOARD BOX SUPPORTED ON SCRAPWOOD, BEERCANS ETC., FOR LEGS. FACE UNDERSIDE WITH BACOFOIL

FINE MESH OVER AIR EXIT HOLES

PUNCH AIR INLET HOLES ROUND BOTTOM EDGES

60 WATT (MAX.) LIGHT BULB IN BATTEN HOLDER

12 IN. SQUARE X 1 IN. BLOCK OR CHIPBOARD BASE

DO NOT LET BULB COME TOO CLOSE TO BOTTOM OF BOX

upper colour when applied by brush. In cases like this, it is far better to spray on the second colour (in fact it is probably true to say that in general it is *always* better to spray any paint finish if you can).

Other areas where this "softening" can be a problem are in the application of fuel-proofing. Tufkote is far better sprayed, for it can soften cellulose base colours, causing them to drag with the brush. Furthermore it is not really feasible to apply Tufkote thin enough by brush to enable it to be applied over enamels without them "pickling", resulting in a nasty mess. Again, with mixed finishing great care needs to be exercised. The same problems are encountered using Hobbypoxy clear as a final surface lacquer. It is possible to apply cellulose over enamel or Tufkote over enamel or use many other incompatible mixes *providing* that several light mist coats are *sprayed* on and *allowed to dry thoroughly between coats.*

If in doubt, always try out mixed finish routes on a scrap piece of the subject first and stick to spraying the "many light coats . . . "!

For simplicity there is much to recommend sticking to one common brand of paint for any one model, but, of course, there are always those of us who like to live dangerously, and let us not forget that there are worthwhile advantages to be found by mixing finishes if we get it right. For example, camouflaging a Spitfire in cellulose and then using matt enamels to apply the roundels, squadron codes etc. means that any errors or blemishes can be removed with a soft tissue and white spirit (the thinner for matt enamels) for this thinner does not affect the cellulose base coat.

Colour Matching

This brings us neatly round to the subject of colour matching (for the camouflage and the markings). Many manufacturers go to extreme lengths to produce "authentic" shades of paint and this is particularly noticeable among the small tinlets and jars of enamels. Most of this research is based on standard colour specifications laid down by the various authorities during the manufacture of the real thing. Others subscribe to the theory that a small model finished in the same shade as the original looks wrong, for it fails to take into account colour perspective. Colour perspective, sometimes referred to as "scale colour", is an illusion caused by looking at distant objects through a less than clear atmosphere. It is a principle that has been followed by artists for centuries. An artist paints what he sees from the distance from which he sees it and it is *not* the colour he would have seen had he been in close proximity to the subject.

In general terms, colour perspective tends to make colours at a dis-

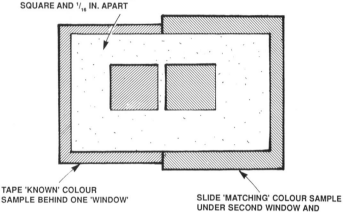

PIECE OF 'NEUTRAL' COLOUR
MASKING CARD - GREY IS BEST.
AVOID BLACK OR WHITE. CUT
TWO HOLES TYPICALLY 1 IN.
SQUARE AND $^1/_{16}$ IN. APART

COLOUR MATCHING TO 'KNOWN' EXAMPLE

TAPE 'KNOWN' COLOUR
SAMPLE BEHIND ONE 'WINDOW'

SLIDE 'MATCHING' COLOUR SAMPLE
UNDER SECOND WINDOW AND
COMPARE WITH KNOWN SAMPLE

MANY CAR PAINT FACTORS USE COLOUR MATCHING
BOOKS THAT WORK ON A SIMILAR PRINCIPLE

tance "appear" to be a shade or two lighter and this is immediately apparent if a sample of card coloured with "real" paint is held at arm's length and compared with a larger panel of card covered in the same paint some tens of feet away.

As an example, a 1/72nd model viewed from a foot away has the same perspective appearance as the real thing viewed from a distance of 72 feet. This technique is used a lot by more fastidious modellers who then either mix their own paints or "modify" existing colours to suit. Remember, though, that the painted sample must be dry (wet paint always appears to be a different colour) and of the same surface finish as the original: matt and gloss paints do not reflect the same amount of light and therefore appear to be different shades. After all, it is the "appearance" that is considered crucial. Of course, in any argument there is always more than one viewpoint and it could be argued that few full-size vehicles retain their pristine condition in service and that one is not always privy to examining the original in the first place. As we saw earlier, poor stirring of the paint used on the full-size more often than not produced "off" shades. Another danger – having visited a famous air museum and seen a restored W.W.2 fighter being painted with Humbrol "authenticolour" and stencilled in "Letraset" I'm not altogether sure how far to believe the evidence of our own eyes.

So while the "experts" will match to perspective, others will accept

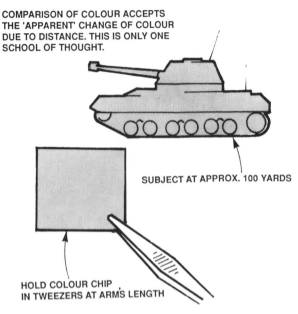

COMPARISON OF COLOUR ACCEPTS THE 'APPARENT' CHANGE OF COLOUR DUE TO DISTANCE. THIS IS ONLY ONE SCHOOL OF THOUGHT.

SUBJECT AT APPROX. 100 YARDS

HOLD COLOUR CHIP IN TWEEZERS AT ARMS LENGTH

full-size shades and there can be no denying the fact that ready availability is an added bonus.

For the flying modeller, however, life is not so easy, for few auto dealers carry matt camouflage cellulose. They *will* match of course, providing that you have a sample (painted on white card from a tinlet!) or one can use epoxides.

Hobbypoxy's range of epoxy colours appears at first glance to be somewhat limited. However, the main colours can be intermixed and stored (provided that no hardener is added) and to this end they have produced a colour mix chart for most of the better known camouflage colours and national marking and insignia colours.

Mixing to the accuracy required takes care and can be made much easier if one invests in a packet of disposable hyperdermic syringes (needles not required).

Temperature
Before we move on to the application techniques with paint perhaps here is the place to consider one other aspect that affects both the handling and the application of paints. It has already been stated that cold and frost can damage paint in storage. So can too much heat! Keep paint warm in winter and cool in summer. When applying paint, remember those points about curing and evaporation and if you are forced to work in inclement environments, maximise on those special

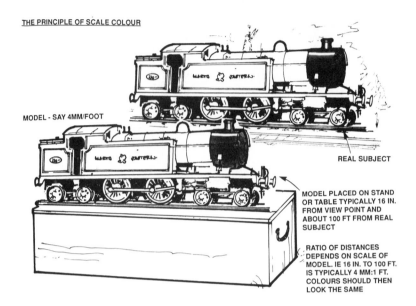

THE PRINCIPLE OF SCALE COLOUR

MODEL - SAY 4MM/FOOT

REAL SUBJECT

MODEL PLACED ON STAND OR TABLE TYPICALLY 16 IN. FROM VIEW POINT AND ABOUT 100 FT FROM REAL SUBJECT

RATIO OF DISTANCES DEPENDS ON SCALE OF MODEL. IE 16 IN. TO 100 FT. IS TYPICALLY 4 MM:1 FT. COLOURS SHOULD THEN LOOK THE SAME

additives mentioned earlier to increase or decrease drying times relative to local temperatures. Wherever possible try to avoid painting in the damp or high humidity levels.

Finally, before moving onto the basic painting techniques, spare a thought for health and safety. Most solvents and thinners are volatile and inflammable. Don't mix or apply paints near naked flame. Epoxides are carcinogenic – use them with care. Some two-part acrylics contain cyanide – again use with caution. Never pour dirty thinners down the sink, toilet or drain, it is illegal and dangerous. If doing a lot of spraying, invest in a simple, reliable face mask. In fact, treat the health and safety aspect as seriously as the colour match, or the stirring of the paint – after all, it's *your* health and the safety of your family.

5 APPLICATION

By now one should be well equipped with paints, primers, brushes, spray kit et al and it is time to consider the application to the model. Now I'm sure that I need not repeat that painting, like many other aspects of modelling, is an area where practice makes perfect. Would-be users of spray or airbrush equipment in particular *need* this practice *first*, and are strongly recommend to read and follow the practice steps set out in the *Airbrushing and Spray Painting Manual* also from Argus Books. In fact it could be argued that the purchase of a couple of cheap plastic kits upon which to practise any form of painting is a sound investment in both time and money.

Of course, the natural-born artists among us will quickly become skilled in the freehand application of paint across a broad range of subject matter. What concerns us here, however, is that vast army of incompetents who, like me, need every assistance they can get from artificial aids to painting.

Now assuming that the model has been properly prepared, primered and coloured with the base colour, the next major step is usually the application of some contrasting colour. In many cases this will have a "soft" feathered edge and with a good airbrush this can be achieved freehand. With a cheaper airbrush it might not be possible to achieve a fine enough "overspray" to obtain satisfactory results and to this end – enter the mask!

Masking

Masks for soft edge camouflage patterns may be cut from stiff bond paper, and supported on scraps of balsa sheet – say 3/32in. for 1/72nd scales up to ½in. for flying models. Spraying over the edge of these paper masks, even with coarse devices such as aerosols, can often produce quite surprising results. Masking in one form or another is the "be-all-and-end-all" of painting to those of us who, like me, are unsteady of hand. It is the *only* way to get straight line edges, constant radius corners and all the plethora of painted detail.

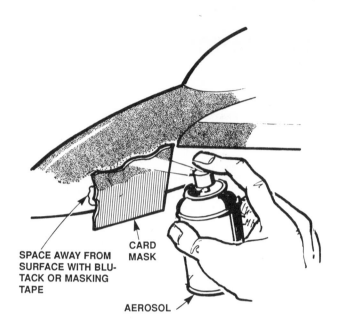

SPACE AWAY FROM
SURFACE WITH BLU-
TACK OR MASKING
TAPE

CARD
MASK

AEROSOL

FOR LARGE SPRAY GUNS AND/OR AEROSOLS
CUT RANDOM SHAPE HOLE IN CARD MASK
AND HOLD MASK BETWEEN $1/_8$ IN. (1:72 SCALE)
AND 1 IN. (FLYING MODELS) FROM SURFACE
TO DIFFUSE THE EDGE

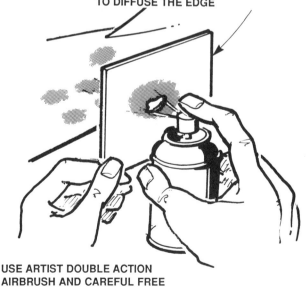

USE ARTIST DOUBLE ACTION
AIRBRUSH AND CAREFUL FREE
HAND FOR BEST RESULTS

Basically masking consists of:
1) Masking tapes
2) Masking film
3) Liquid masks
4) Paper masks
and all four have a specific part to play in good painting.

Masking Tapes Masking tape to most of us is the pale creamy coloured crepe paper stuff, usually 1in. wide, and used primarily by full-
size sprayers. This is a very general description and needs further
explanation. First off let us consider the adhesive. Now there is
"sticky" and there is "sticky" and any tape manufacturer worth his salt
will produce a range of tapes with differing degrees of "tack" – the
proper description of the stickiness of the tape. Post Office-proof parcel tape should go on and stay on, defying the most ardent attempts
by the G.P.O. to get it off, but masking tape, on the other hand, must
go on and peel off again without damage to the surface to which it was
stuck. Consequently it pays to shop around the differing suppliers to

**Rub-down lettering and sheet colour film and fine-line masking tape (down to
.010 in.) are among offerings from Chartpak.**

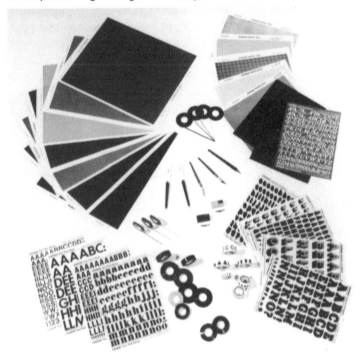

find a tape having a sufficiently "low tack". Sellotape in its generic form does not make good masking tape, although if really pushed it *can* be used. Taking the tape and pulling it over the edge of the table sticky side down will remove much of the adhesive quality and when you've got the hang of how much to remove, it can make a reasonable substitute for the real thing.

Crêpe paper masking tape has a degree of stretch but not enough to make it negotiate curved surfaces easily. The trick here is to invest in a cutting mat. These self healing plastic mats are of immense use in all aspects of modelling and in this instance, 1in. wide tape can be stuck down to the mat and stripped into narrower widths using a steel straight edge and a sharp modelling knife. These thin strips can be used to outline the painted area and if the strips are kept to 1/8in. or narrower then they will negotiate compound curves with ease. Now use short pieces of 1in. tape or similar and torn newspaper to cover up the rest of the model and you are home and dry. Apart from the standard ½, ¾, 1 and 2in. widths of masking tape commonly found in D.I.Y. motorists' stores, shopping from the specialist custom car dealers (even if it means shopping by mail) will yield reels of narrow cut tape 1/16, 3/32 and 1/8in. wide. If you are doing a lot of masking this is a great deal more convenient than cutting short lengths to size!

Later on it will become apparent that there are several short cuts that can be taken when masking and many if not all of these rely on masking tape cut to some given, specific width. This can be difficult to do (and time-consuming) if a very accurate width is called for. Once

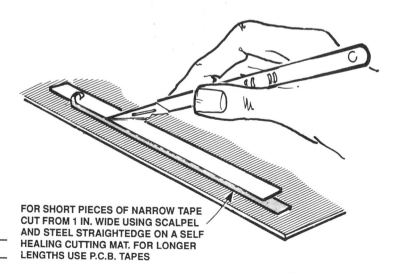

FOR SHORT PIECES OF NARROW TAPE CUT FROM 1 IN. WIDE USING SCALPEL AND STEEL STRAIGHTEDGE ON A SELF HEALING CUTTING MAT. FOR LONGER LENGTHS USE P.C.B. TAPES

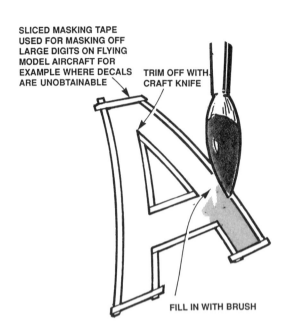

SLICED MASKING TAPE USED FOR MASKING OFF LARGE DIGITS ON FLYING MODEL AIRCRAFT FOR EXAMPLE WHERE DECALS ARE UNOBTAINABLE

TRIM OFF WITH CRAFT KNIFE

FILL IN WITH BRUSH

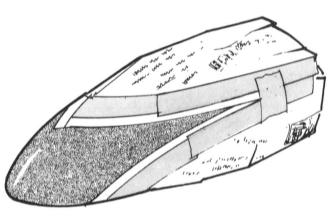

MASKING A DUAL-CURVED
SUBJECT WITH NARROW TAPE,
THEN WIDER TAPE AND NEWSPAPER

more, the fact that we orbit on the edge of somebody else's industry provides us with the answer to the problem.

Good graphics and drawing office suppliers will be able to offer you "black" crepe masking tapes in a vast range of widths from as narrow as 10 thou to as wide as 2in. in both imperial and metric sizes. This type of tape is used in the printed circuit board industry to produce the master artwork from which the final P.C.B. is photographically reproduced. Tape is used rather than ink due to the fact that during artwork production it often becomes necessary to peel off the line and re-position it, not easy with an ink line! Of course modern computer-aided design does away with this chore, but at present there are many layouts still done by hand. Because the width of a printed circuit track is directly related to its current carrying capacity, the designer will often need several widths, hence the wide variety available. Names such as Letraset, Mecanorma and Chartpak are in this business.

Sometimes a quite complex shape is required and to this end it may not be very practical to mask off the model in situ. Providing such a shape is reasonably small, placing 2in. tape sticky side down onto a cutting mat allows the luxury of drawing the shape onto the tape. From here it becomes a simple matter to cut the shape out of the tape. Carefully lifting the tape (with the cut hole in it) from the mat and positioning it onto the model will allow the relevant area to be painted.

Masking Films Apart from masking tape, probably the next widest usage is that of masking films. More often than not this is referred to as "Frisk film". Frisk is to film what Biro is to ball pens and Hoover is to vacuum cleaners, and many brands are currently available from such household names as Badger and Magic Marker to those specialist graphics suppliers such as Frisk and Mecanorma.

Masking films are, by and large, thin, transparent plastic sheet with a low tack adhesive on one side, protected on the sticky side by a backing sheet. Films can be glossy or matt surfaced, the matt being preferred where a shape or design has to be drawn onto the film, for the matt surface takes pencil, ballpoint or felt tip pens extremely well.

In general, the trick is to peel off the protective backing and stick the film to the model. Cut out carefully the area to be painted and remove the film from that area. Store the removed portion of film on the backing sheet. Now carefully paint in the "hole" in the film, taking particular care to ensure that the film edges are rubbed well down to avoid paint creepage. Film is intended primarily for airbrush work (as of course are tapes) but if approached with caution, paint applied by brush, thinly and almost dry, will work as a second best.

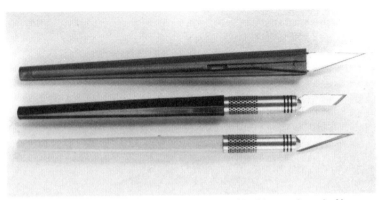

Chartpak market excellent stencil-cutting knives, ideal for mask work. Also useful as rather up-market modelling knives!

When the paint is dry simply remove the film. For multiple colour work, say red, white and blue aircraft insignia, the stored cut-out film may be replaced in its hole, covering up the painted area, and the neighbouring piece of film removed for the application of the next adjacent colour and so on. Quite complex multi-coloured artwork such as squadron crests on aircraft or corporate logos on large scale model railway engines can be achieved quickly and simply by using this multiple "cut–peel–paint–replace" film technique.

Of course nothing is perfect in this imperfect world and film masking does have its snags. First of all, film is best on flat surfaces and will not handle compound curves. Nor will it adhere to, say, a heavily rivet-detailed plastic kit. Furthermore, the adhesive on the rear of the film has an affinity for certain types of paint and when the film is removed one may well find traces of adhesive left on the model. This can be removed by using proprietary art cleaning solutions such as Scotch Clean Art from 3M. On no account use thinners or general modelling solvents which will almost certainly remove the paint as well!

Despite these snags, film masking is of tremendous use and is well worth investigating fully. Most masking films are available from good art shops in packets of cut sheet to the usual "paper" sizes, i.e. A4, A3 etc., but can also be bought on the roll, which is usually cheaper in terms of pence per unit area and also allows larger masks to be made.

Masking Fluids (or Liquid Masks)

To the average modeller this means Humbrol Maskol, but there are other brands within the model industry and still other brands used in, say, the custom car business. Predominantly these films are formed

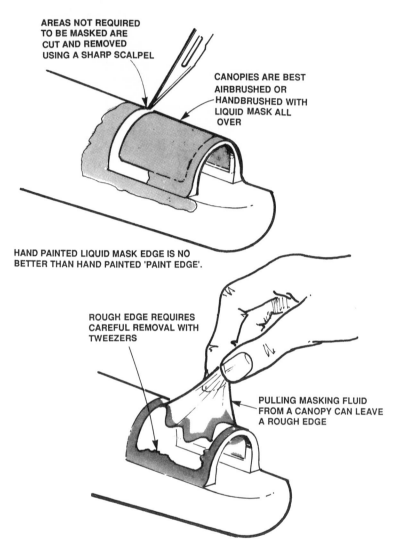

AREAS NOT REQUIRED
TO BE MASKED ARE
CUT AND REMOVED
USING A SHARP SCALPEL

CANOPIES ARE BEST
AIRBRUSHED OR
HANDBRUSHED WITH
LIQUID MASK ALL
OVER

HAND PAINTED LIQUID MASK EDGE IS NO
BETTER THAN HAND PAINTED 'PAINT EDGE'.

ROUGH EDGE REQUIRES
CAREFUL REMOVAL WITH
TWEEZERS

PULLING MASKING FLUID
FROM A CANOPY CAN LEAVE
A ROUGH EDGE

by the air drying (evaporation) of latex-based products. They can be applied by paint-brush or by spray and dry quickly to a thin film.

Most modellers apply liquid masks to cockpit canopies and other transparencies by paint brush, covering the clear areas that have to remain unpainted. Airbrushing or brush painting over the whole then paints the frames only. When dry, the masks can be removed by lifting the film with the point of a modelling knife and peeling off. Be careful here, though, for the film from liquid masking is much more flexible than other forms of mask and can easily tear or stretch to the point where the adhered paint flakes off and sticks to the other areas of the model.

The major snag with applying liquid films by brush like this is that the masked edge is only as good as one's free-hand with the brush. In which case, why not just paint the frames freehand in the first place? The best approach with liquid masking is to apply it all over the relevant area in a smooth even coat. Of course this is more likely to be even if it is sprayed on, taking good care to clean the airbrush/spray gun thoroughly before the liquid goes off inside the nozzle. When the mask has dried to an even film, simply cut out the unwanted mask area with a sharp knife, as with Frisk film. This approach will provide a much sharper edge over which to paint. Multiple-colour images can be dealt with in the same manner as with Frisk film, except that the flexible nature of liquid mask films prohibits the storage and replacement of peeled-off areas. Here then, it simply becomes a case of allowing the paint to dry before re-coating the relevant area with another layer of liquid.

Liquid masking is perhaps a little more fiddly than film masks (due to the drying time etc.) but does have the advantage that it can be used on compound curves and uneven surfaces. It is often to be found in use by the better car customisers, and I have seen a Transit van "muralled" in this manner. Ever wondered how these murals seem so photographic in appearance? Well, this van was sprayed with liquid mask and a photographic slide projector used to project a colour picture onto the side of the van. Multiple "in-situ" cuts in the mask were made and painted with many re-coats of the mask as the job progressed. Finally, all of the mask was removed and the final detail and soft edge shading added freehand. Try that one on your model – it really works!

Of course time is of the very essence in jobs of this nature and modellers tend, by and large, to rush at painting jobs with the inevitable results.

Paper Masks Paper masks are perhaps the most useful yet least used of all masking techniques. Like all masks they benefit from the application of the paint by spray, but used carefully, they can still work with a paint-brush. Cutting paper stencils requires only a sharp knife and a cutting mat and, of course, the paper. In many cases where a decorative pattern, or perhaps just the name of the model, is required to be painted on, say, the wing of a model airplane, the design can be schemed out on the full-size plan in pencil or felt tipped pens until the exact shape and size has been obtained. Photocopying this plan then enables a cut paper stencil to be made from the photocopy (better than cutting up the original plan).

Such a paper stencil can also be made for an enormous range of lettering. Invest in a Letraset or Meccanorma catalogue – it's worth the few pounds that it costs. Within these catalogues are literally hundreds of different letter styles. Of course rub-down lettering of this style does not come cheap, nor does it come in every size or, for that matter, in every colour. However, once the letter style has been chosen, simply visit your local copy shop and have the page enlarged a couple of times. Now cut out the relevant letters and paste them together to make the words or names. Let your imagination run riot. Words don't *always* look best in a straight line! Experiment with slopes and angles or even "uneven" lines of letters. Once you've got the words all stuck down, re-visit the copy shop and enlarge the word to fit the model and bingo, you have a copy already to cut out to make your paper stencil! Alternatively you can work with tracing paper, tracing each letter in turn into its correct place, then copying up to size. Most High Street copy shops will be happy to copy up or down in size for quite a modest fee and some of them might even be interested to find out what you are doing.

Cutting out a paper stencil presupposes that one knows how to use it! In many cases the stencil can simply be held in place with the fingers and sprayed over, the air pressure from the airbrush or spray gun effectively keeping the paper in contact with the model. This trick tends not to work with complex lettering, particularly when letters have middles like "O", "B", "D", etc. or where quite complex shapes are required. Equally, of course, it doesn't work for paint-brushing.

Working with photocopies for stencils is easy from the production point of view for it involves no freehand drawing – a factor that is of great asset to those of us who can't draw. But if photocopiers were self-adhesive like Frisk film all our problems would disappear. This is not as stupid as it seems, for as we have seen before, a lot of the specialist products aimed at the graphic artist are of immeasurable use to us as well. Aerosols of light adhesive such as Scotch Spray Mount (in the blue tin) made for temporarily fixing photos and drawings during artwork preparation are ideal for our use. These are latex-based adhesives that can be lightly sprayed over the back of the stencil (including all of the pre-cut middles of letters and patterns) effectively adding a sticky back virtually the same as Frisk film. Now it becomes only a matter of correct alignment, pressing down and painting over.

Of course it is fairly glib to talk about "just cut out your film, tape, photocopy etc. with a sharp knife". In many cases a modelling knife with a sharp blade is all that is needed, but in some instances there are particular reasons for not using such a knife. A trip to your art shop again will reveal a range of specialist tools for the working of these materials. Stencil knives come in a range of shapes and sizes to suit individual needs and for cutting complex curved stencils a swivel knife will pay dividends. The blade in a swivel knife, as its name implies, is not fixed, but pivots around the longitudinal axis of the knife so that the blade turns as it follows the curved path that is being cut. First tries with knives of this type usually end in disaster until one finds out how and when the blade moves to produce smooth flowing curved cuts; once mastered it is an extremely useful tool.

For those less gifted in the arts, like myself, the steel rule, set square, protractor, compasses etc. etc. of our schoolboy geometry days will assist in getting stencils square, round etc. and to this end a good set of geometry or draughtsman's tools can be a worthwhile asset. Initial outlay is not heavy but if, as in my case, you expect to do a fair amount of model painting, then it is worthwhile considering one of the more adventurous sets. My set enables me to draw circles in pencil, draughtsman's pen and ink, felt tip pens and even has a swivel knife that fits the compasses for the accurate cutting of circles in Frisk film and similar. No more, therefore, the ragged edge to my Spitfire markings!

Earlier on in this chapter reference was made to catalogue of the Letraset, Meccanorma etc. companies who specialise in rub-down lettering. Now while the majority of model decoration is done with

Hand-painted transfers on gummed labels treated with Micro-Superfilm. The gum sticks the painted film to the model.

paints and a brush, there is little point in doing it all the hard way if short cuts can be found. In many cases small lettering on models can be done directly with Letraset or one of the other proprietary brands and while these lettering sheets are not cheap, the time saved and the accuracy achieved can often outweigh the costs. Some specialist suppliers to the model trade produce specific sets of rub-down markings to suit individual models and if this applies to your model, thank your lucky stars, put away your paint-brush and use them! Waterslide and Methfix types of transfer should also not be passed by, for where applicable they save a lot of time, not to mention the frustration brought about by having to hand-paint these markings. Further details of how to get the best out of these specialist accessories will be found in the following chapters dealing more with specific kinds of model. One trick well worth mentioning here is the painting of "home-made" transfers, not a difficult task.

When working on models for which commercial transfers are not available it is always possible to paint on the markings and insignia by hand, whether with a steady freehand paint-brush or cleverly masked spraying.

However, any error or blemish in the markings is on the model and usually spells disaster. If one could do this painting off the model then mistakes could be scrapped and a new insignia started until a good one did emerge. At this stage the marking – complete and perfect – can be transferred to the model. There are spin-offs from this technique too. First of all one can work on a flat table or drawing board with compasses, pens, rule etc. (much easier than working on the model!) which enables greater accuracy to be achieved much more easily. Secondly, as has just been stated, if it goes wrong you can scrap it and start again without damage to the model. Now there is a great psychological advantage in the knowledge that it does not matter if you screw up the first, second or third attempt – you are bound to get it right eventually. With this knowledge, the pressure is off and more often than not the very first attempt comes out right.

Home-made transfers can be tackled in several ways. One of the simplest is to overpaint existing transfers of the correct size but perhaps wrong colour or style. Matt enamel is favourite for this, applied by pen, brush or spray.

Failing this, obtain some "empty" transfer sheet, i.e. where only the backing clear lacquer has been printed but no colour. This can then be painted by hand or by stencil as above. This type of "no-colour" transfer sheet is available from one or two specialist retail model outfits or can often be obtained from the major silk screen transfer printers (see your yellow pages or local Thompson directory).

A third option is to use old-fashioned gummed paper parcel labels. Here it is simply a case of brushing or spraying a couple of coats of clear lacquer onto the gummed side of the label. When dry paint the markings onto the lacquer and presto – instant transfers.

Transfers, in general, prefer to be stuck to shiny, smooth models and require only careful trimming to their outlines to provide a professional appearance. Some models, though, will have heavy surface detail, rivets, panel lines etc. that interfere with the correct adhesion of the transfer. Once again, reference to the specialist manufacturers helps. One such product line is the Micro system consisting of gloss and flat lacquers for preparation and finishing, together with Microset and Microsol transfer fixatives. Use of these specialist products will work wonders on your transfers, softening the ink/paint/carrier film and enabling the transfer to "go soft" and pull down over minor surface irregularities.

We now turn to points arising in areas of specific interest, but it is hoped that readers will not by-pass a chapter simply because its subject matter does not appeal. There is a lot to be learned and it is surprising how many useful little hints and tips may be picked up from other modellers' problems.

What's all about. An electric-powered R/C *Spitfire* with an excellent paint finish by the author.

6 FLYING MODEL AIRCRAFT

Because a model of this sort is expected to perform well in the air, it *must not* be overweight. Short cuts on structural complexity become a necessity, simplicity often being the name of the game. One upshot of this is that scale model aircraft rarely follow full-size structural practice and consequently one may find sheet balsa wood replacing sheet metal, or balsa sheet replacing fabric over an open structure. If the structure cannot duplicate the full-size then the paint job has to create the illusion of the full-size and thereby fool the onlooker. Even on non-scale models a bright and colourful surface finish is pleasing to the eye and may even be essential to good visual orientation when airborne: a pale grey or white model all but disappears into the sky on a cold winter's day. So colour and the application of colour take on a new meaning. Furthermore, the weight of the applied paint finish must also be borne in mind, for any increase in weight will reduce performance and the required finished result must therefore be achieved in the lightest possible way.

We should accept at this stage that the correct amount and type of prefinishing has been carried out and we are now at the colouring stage (see Chapter 3).

In general, radio-controlled and control-line models can be lumped together here, for much of the finishing technique will be common. For the scale afficionado camouflage may well be high on the priority list, and has been seen already, soft edge work is best achieved by spraying (no matter how amateur the equipment!). Hard edge division will rely on one of the masking systems already discussed and multiple colours can be dealt with by using Frisk film.

However, there are many tips and hints that can be picked up along the way, most of which are valid in one area or other. Brush painting of camouflage is never easy but the careful use of a stippling brush can "fudge" the edge of the colour to create a ragged division. Rather than spend money on a specialist stippling brush, it is just as effective to take an old paint-brush, whose tip is a bit past it, and cut the bristles off about half way up, leaving *all* of the bristles the same length. This

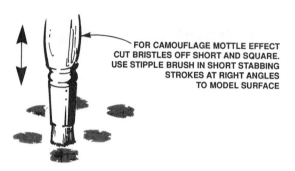

FOR CAMOUFLAGE MOTTLE EFFECT
CUT BRISTLES OFF SHORT AND SQUARE.
USE STIPPLE BRUSH IN SHORT STABBING
STROKES AT RIGHT ANGLES
TO MODEL SURFACE

brush is then used with the bristles at right angles to the model to "dab" the wet edge to the paint line and gently blur it. Of course, like all special techniques there is much to recommend the practice of trying it all out first on some scrap material.

Adding the markings to a scale model can once again often rely on careful masking, but do not lose sight of the old-fashioned method of a pen and rule or compasses. Just because a technique has been around for a while does not mean that it isn't valid. Pens and compasses were featured in Chapter 2 and should not be overlooked here, not only on military or other scale models but also as a basis for decorating non-scale sports models. One of the areas that frighten modellers is the fear of ruining the paintwork when the model is almost complete and as we have seen already, there is much to commend the use of home-made transfers and working "off the model".

However, there are many occasions where this is not practical, or indeed possible, and then there is no choice but to paint directly on the model's surface. Even here there are ways to help and one useful safety measure involves the use of barrier lacquer. Suppose, for instance, that it is intended to apply a mural to the wing of a model. First apply the base colour, say, in cellulose, and let it dry thoroughly, ensuring that there will be no entrapment of solvents at the next stage. Now give the wing one good coat of fuel proofer (Tufkote works well here!). Again allow to dry thoroughly. Apply the mural using Humbrol (or similar) matt enamels. The reasoning is simple – matt enamels dry fast so that you can see what you are doing, and furthermore they can easily be wiped clean with white spirit should you make a mistake. White spirit does not attack Tufkote Q.E.D.! When completely finished, recoat with Tufkote to seal it all in. Clear Hobbypoxy works just as well and is as easy to use. Like all model painting, it pays to spray on these barrier lacquers but careful brushwork is usually

Very often one can't actually see what you are doing until the first coat of grey primer is applied. This shows up all the blemishes and areas needing further work. This near-scale Hawker Hurricane has been primered and the areas still needing work treated with Squadron "Greenstuff", a filling and finishing putty well loved by the plastic kit brigade.

Traditionally tissue paper and dope finish used on balsa wood. Many coats of dope and much elbow grease needed. Technique being gently replaced by modern finishing resins.

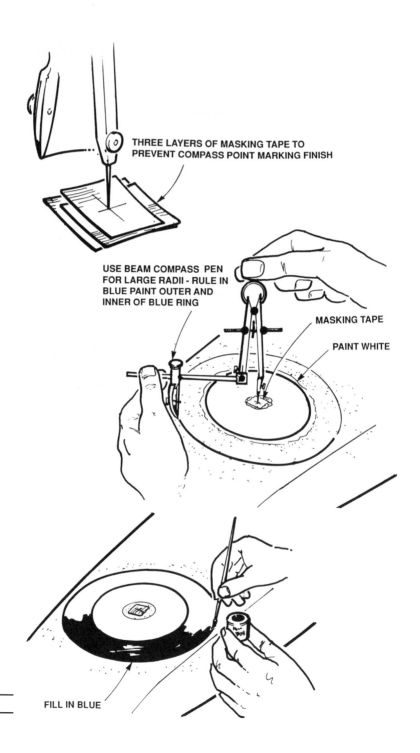

THREE LAYERS OF MASKING TAPE TO PREVENT COMPASS POINT MARKING FINISH

USE BEAM COMPASS PEN FOR LARGE RADII - RULE IN BLUE PAINT OUTER AND INNER OF BLUE RING

MASKING TAPE

PAINT WHITE

FILL IN BLUE

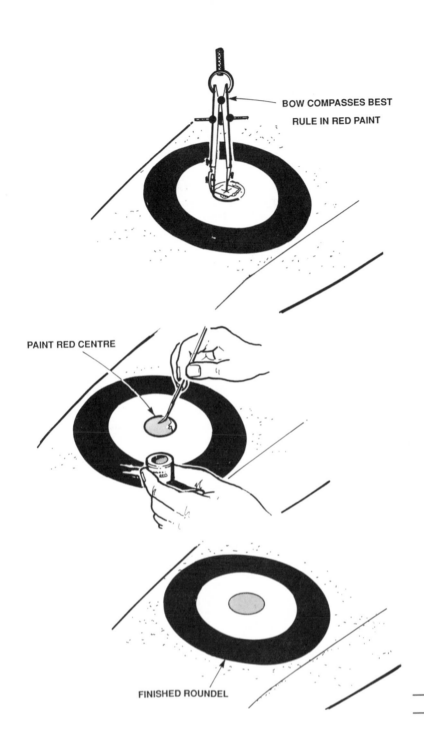

BOW COMPASSES BEST
RULE IN RED PAINT

PAINT RED CENTRE

FINISHED ROUNDEL

acceptable. As in any situation, having a good escape route like this usually means that you do nothing wrong when applying the matt enamel – mistakes only tend to happen when you have positively no way of rectification. This barrier lacquer technique is equally valid on all models and makes life just as easy for, say, the scale afficionado applying his multi-coloured squadron badge freehand.

Film and Paint Matching

Few of us are budding artists and when it comes to freehand decoration it pays to look around one to see what ideas can be pinched from elsewhere. Sometimes with a kit the box art helps and provides a colourful subject, but even here one can be caught between two stools. While not specifically a subject for this book, it may be helpful to make a passing reference to the widespread use of heat shrink films in covering today's models. Few if any paints stick properly to these films, whose very nature is to shrug off all attempts of dirt and other materials to cling to them. Not even the specialist paints made expressly for use with, say, Solarfilm, Coverite or Monokote, really adhere well. Solarlac, the matching colour range of paints for Solarfilm, is best kept for its intended use of painting the non-film parts of the model to match (or to contrast with) the parts that *are* film covered. Solarlac is colour-matched to the Solarfilm range of colours and also to that of the Hobbypoxy range. The thinking here is to allow the mixed finishing of models, say a painted glass-fibre fuselage and a film-covered wing and tail. Colour trim can then be added to match.

This mix 'n match system can be easily demonstrated by my "Argo". This high quality motor glider from the West German Robbe company *was* painted and filmed to match the box art (not a usual occurrence as most of my models tend to finish up a bit "way out"). The elegant lines of the "Argo" are brought about by a sleek moulded

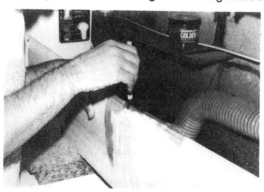

Stippling brush – used for stippling action when applying resin to glass cloth while prefinishing wing. Note upright use of brush. Same technique can be used to apply mottle camouflage to WW2 vehicles.

plastic fuselage, yet the wings and tail use the accepted modern approach of veneered foam. Wings and tail just cry out for the Solarfilm treatment which would not be suited to the fuselage which really just has to be painted. In such a situation this film/paint matching system is of extreme value.

Surface preparation of the fuselage involved a complete rub down with wet-and-dry to remove all traces of mould release wax and to reveal the blemishes where the mould join line occurred. These blemishes were subsequently filled with a proprietary hobby filler (actually Squadron Green stuff, a cellulose-based filler more usually found in the plastic kit enthusiast's tool box!) and rubbed down again. Two coats of grey cellulose primer were sprayed on from an aerosol can that I just happened to have to hand. As Hobbypoxy was to be used for the colour coats, then Hobbypoxy primer would have done just as well, in fact probably better, for as has been said before, if in doubt, stick to the same brand throughout. Top coat was Hobbypoxy gloss white, not chosen for its fuel-proof qualities, for the "Argo" is electrically propelled, but for the fact that it is the nearest that I've ever come to matching white Solarfilm. You'd be surprised at just how many shades of white there are!

Now the wings, tail and fuselage were all white and this is where the problems started, for the box art shows red and blue trim on wings, tail, *and* fuselage. Bearing in mind the difficulty of getting paint to remain on film, the wings and tail were trimmed with "Solartrim" a self-adhesive stick-on trim sheet that can be cut to shape and pattern, and simply stuck in place. This product also matches both the range of film colours and that of Hobbypoxy paint. Consequently the fuselage could be masked and painted.

Of course the crunch comes when the entire model is assembled, for the fin is integrally moulded with the fuselage (and is therefore painted) while the rudder is film and trim. Just how well the colours match at the hinge line has to be seen to be believed, with many a viewer convinced that the fin and rudder are *both* painted.

The box art, however, may not appeal and many modellers like to individualise their models. To this end it is worth taking time out to scheme the colours carefully. Don't be afraid of cheating! Copy and adapt is the name of the game. If you see something that catches the imagination, remember it, or the parts of it that really attract, and incorporate it in your next scheme. Don't be afraid to move toward the arty-crafty. Too many colour schemes are stereotyped: try to move away from the norm. Investigate pastel shades or car type metallics for a change. Scheme the shades to match. For instance, pick a dark prime

STRIPES AND CHEQUERS

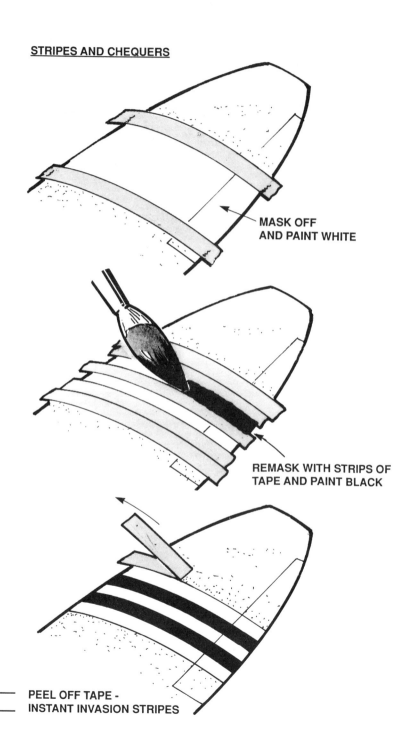

MASK OFF
AND PAINT WHITE

REMASK WITH STRIPS OF
TAPE AND PAINT BLACK

PEEL OFF TAPE -
INSTANT INVASION STRIPES

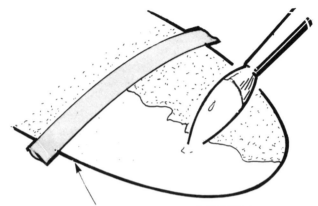

MASK OFF AND PAINT WHITE

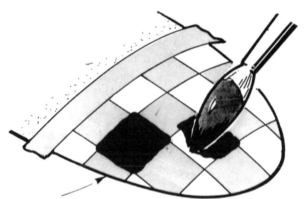

**COVER WITH TAPE OR FILM AND CUT SQUARES.
REMOVE EVERY OTHER SQUARE MASK**

**PEEL OFF ALL MASKS
TO REVEAL CHEQUERS**

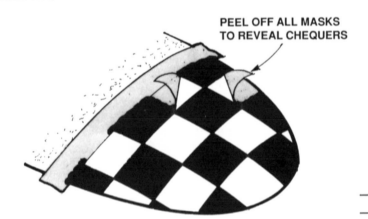

colour (not primary colour, but a colour of your choice) say dark metallic chocolate. Now buy a can of white and collect some empty jars (with lids). Decant enough white to cover the entire model into a jar and add just a few drops of brown to make a cream colour for the all-over colour. Mix brown and white 50% each to give a milk chocolate effect for detail and lettering and use the original dark brown for outlines and highlights. This results in a clever blend of matching shades that looks like you've really bothered rather than just chucking any old colour all over the model.

Tape Edges If you brush paint, try to take extra care to avoid paint creeping under masking tapes. This can usually be done by applying a coat of the base colour over the edge of the tape first (to seal the edge) and then apply the contrasting colour and *always* remember to pull film and tape masks off carefully, pulling back on themselves at 180° rather than pulling off at right angles to the model.

If you spray, whether with aerosols or more sophisticated equipment, remember that you can now shade. So, go for soft edge decoration on at least *one* edge of colour lines.

Of course all this talk of fancy paint jobs bordering on the artistic adds weight and there are many models whose very nature prohibits this addition. Most free flight models, as an example, especially those of the Peanut or other similar small sizes, weigh scant fractions of an ounce all-up and the addition of 100% to this weight by painting is a non-starter.

Consequently in these small sizes one is extremely limited in what one can do. Very often coloured tissue is used to cover the airframe and the barest surface detail (elevators, ailerons etc.), is added with ink in a draughtsman's pen. Artists' inks are sometimes used as, being water soluble, they can be used during the water shrinking stage, but are then difficult to mask as the coloured water tends to bleed along the fibres of the tissue.

Regrettably we are forced to accept that the very minimum amount of paint is the answer in these small sizes, as is the application in thin coats with an airbrush, for it becomes increasingly difficult to cope with paint-brush application within the weight and structural constraints. Having said that, there are those whose skills with an airbrush have enabled them to create all the effect of a metal-skinned and panelled aircraft on a tissue-covered model.

One of the most difficult problems with any form of model aircraft, be it scale or not, radio controlled or peanut, is the problem of handling, in particular how to hold parts for painting. A surprising number of

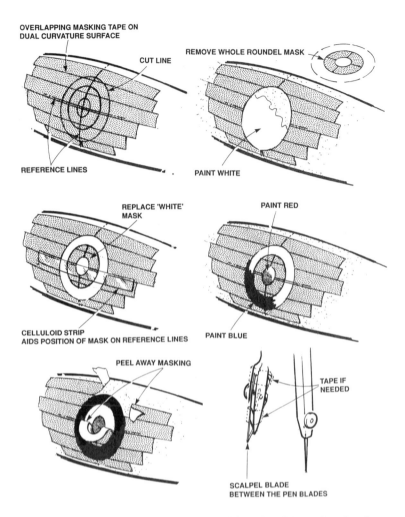

OVERLAPPING MASKING TAPE ON
DUAL CURVATURE SURFACE

CUT LINE

REMOVE WHOLE ROUNDEL MASK

REFERENCE LINES

PAINT WHITE

REPLACE 'WHITE'
MASK

PAINT RED

CELLULOID STRIP
AIDS POSITION OF MASK ON REFERENCE LINES

PAINT BLUE

PEEL AWAY MASKING

TAPE IF
NEEDED

SCALPEL BLADE
BETWEEN THE PEN BLADES

paint finishes are spoilt by the wayward thumb-print or when turning a component round, knocking it on the workshop shelf with the resultant cloud of dust settling. It will pay handsome dividends to make up jigs and fixtures before starting, for endeavouring to hold a model that is wet all over will inevitably lead to spoiled areas.

Once again we see the age-old argument between fast or slow setting paints and brush or spray application. Brush application is obviously limited to the slower drying products, thereby allowing the brushmarks to flow out (see previous chapters). Fast-drying paints really need to be sprayed on. The basic premise is still the same, multiple thin coats being preferred to one thick coat. Yet another

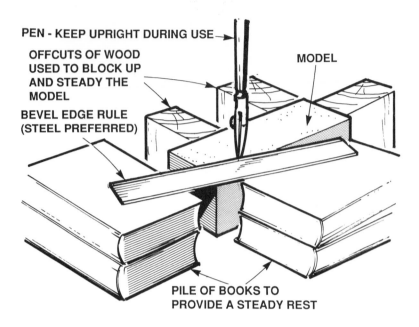

PEN - KEEP UPRIGHT DURING USE

OFFCUTS OF WOOD
USED TO BLOCK UP
AND STEADY THE
MODEL

MODEL

BEVEL EDGE RULE
(STEEL PREFERRED)

PILE OF BOOKS TO
PROVIDE A STEADY REST

handling problem occurs when adding detail by hand (or by brush to satisfy the language purists).

Signwriters and most artists use some sort of hand rest to provide a "steady" when working, most often a mahl-stick for work on vertical surfaces. Use of such a stick support is an acquired art but the painter's "bridge" for horizontal work is not only easy to use, it is quick and easy to produce.

Let us return to the hypothetical Spitfire or similar and consider painting by hand the squadron badge on the fuselage side. First of all prop up the fuselage on the work table, side to be painted uppermost, and then ensure that it cannot move. It might not be practical to clamp the model in place, dependent upon its size, but polythene bags full of wet sand or even earth from the garden will conform to shape and can be used to block the model up and prevent any movement. Now place a pile of encyclopaedias either side of the model to a height where a short plank can be placed across the fuselage, close to its surface and resting on the two piles of books. Resting one's hand and/or forearm on this bridge makes for a much steadier state. Using the inevitable photocopy trace through some carbon paper and transfer the pattern to the model. Now it is just a case of a steady hand, quality brush/pen etc. and the job is complete.

7 OTHER WORKING MODELS

Other working models yield problems in their own right, many of which have quite specific solutions. To a large extent, model boats exhibit similar problems to those of the flying model.

Boats

Boats powered by diesel or glow motors will have the same problems regarding fuel-proofing, although, having said that, exhaust systems in boats differ from those in aircraft and are often directed cleanly away outside of the hull. This tends to reduce by far the problem and if good housekeeping is a function of the operation of a boat little if any neat fuel will be spilt, reducing it still further. The waterproof quality of the paint and its ability to stand the ravages of time and the attack from water pollutants are then the prime requisites, whether the boat is powered by the "infernal combustion engine" or the quiet, clean, electric motor.

Once again the scale model predominates among boat modellers, often exhibiting a degree of intricate detail not found among model aircraft enthusiasts (with the exceptions of the contest breed of course).

Here one can benefit by the use of branded two-pack materials for the hull wherever possible, on the grounds of a better quality, longer lasting, fade-resistant finish. However, the vast amount of fine detail on the deck, superstructure, masts etc. would prove virtually impossible to mask off and spray. In this instance, brush painting provides a better route.

With the exception of submarines, few models subject these upper works to more than a cursory dose of water (or exhaust waste where relevant) and less durable paints can often be used.

The relatively small scales of such craft will bring superstructure detail, crewmen etc. into the same areas as those occupied by the small scale plastics and military enthusiasts to whom the next chapter is addressed.

Non-scale boats are usually restricted to the out-and-out racing and speed classes (although there are quite a few freelance sports models about) and here, as with aircraft, mixed material construction is likely to be found. The answer, again as with aircraft, is to finish each material individually, then reduce the surface to an overall uniformity with one of the proprietary primers, finishing in the normal manner.

Nowadays many kit boats make widespread use of vacuum moulded parts from styrene, A.B.S. or butyrates. Here it is well worth checking out the compatibility of paints chosen with the plastics concerned. Some, like styrene, are apt to melt if cellulose-based colours are applied by heavy-handed use of a paint-brush. Even airbrushing is not the answer, for although the soft mist application no longer destroys the plastic, despite the etching effect of the solvents the paints never really key and can often come off in an entire sheet when removing the subsequent masking tapes. Two courses of action are open here, one being to return to the use of enamels with the attendant problems. The other is to use the newer brands of two-pack primers used in the motor industry. Many of these new formulations have been put together to overcome the inherent problems with today's motor cars of mixed plastic and metal construction and will happily "etch" both metals and plastics equally well. Such primers are ideal for plastic sub-assemblies and being of the high-build variety can also be used to fill blemishes and errors in building.

Cars

Similar problems occur with rigid, opaque plastics used for the bodies of radio controlled model cars and the same alternative action applied.

However, within this field, there is a growing tendency to move towards transparent body shells and here we have a horse of a different

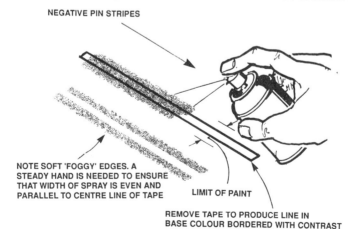

NEGATIVE PIN STRIPES

NOTE SOFT 'FOGGY' EDGES. A STEADY HAND IS NEEDED TO ENSURE THAT WIDTH OF SPRAY IS EVEN AND PARALLEL TO CENTRE LINE OF TAPE

LIMIT OF PAINT

REMOVE TAPE TO PRODUCE LINE IN BASE COLOUR BORDERED WITH CONTRAST

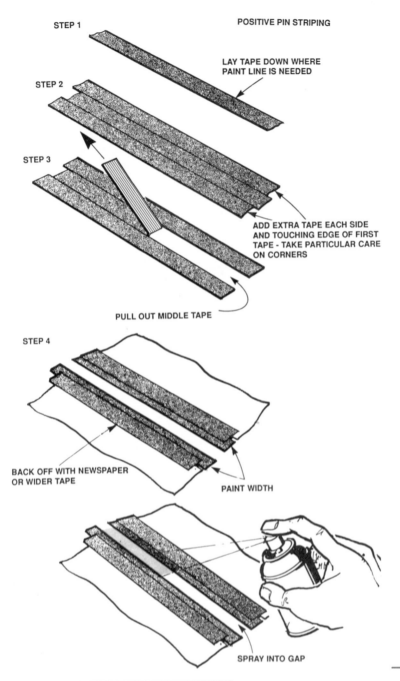

STEP 1

POSITIVE PIN STRIPING

LAY TAPE DOWN WHERE
PAINT LINE IS NEEDED

STEP 2

STEP 3

ADD EXTRA TAPE EACH SIDE
AND TOUCHING EDGE OF FIRST
TAPE - TAKE PARTICULAR CARE
ON CORNERS

PULL OUT MIDDLE TAPE

STEP 4

BACK OFF WITH NEWSPAPER
OR WIDER TAPE

PAINT WIDTH

SPRAY INTO GAP

REMOVE TAPE TO PRODUCE POSITIVE LINE

LARGER MODELS WILL BENEFIT FROM SPECIALLY MADE JIGS OR
COMMERCIAL ITEMS SUCH AS THOSE AVAILABLE FROM A.S.P.

colour. Most of these shells are moulded from polycarbonate plastic or its derivatives. Brand names such as "Lexan" are frequently to be seen in this area of modelling.

Now Lexan and the like exhibit properties much sought after by the model car brigade. First off, it is light in weight and therefore does little to affect the performance and handling of the car. Furthermore it is extremely tough (Lexan is used in anti-vandal situations) and remarkably flexible, enabling it to absorb a great deal of punishment in the hands of the less skilled operator. Unfortunately this flexibility is also its downfall and one needs to understand the complex nature of this plastic to be aware of the pitfalls.

Most plastics of this nature are hydrocarbons i.e. they are made up of complex chemical chains of Hydrogen, Oxygen and Carbon. The exact arrangement of the molecules and the "doctoring" of the chain by adding other substances produce the wide range of plastics currently in use today. Lexan is made very flexible by the addition of such an additional "plasticiser" molecule but the retention that the basic chain has on this additional plasticiser molecule is slight and it takes very little to cause its grip to slacken and the spare molecules drift off. "Plasticiser Migration" is a serious problem with polycarbonates and all sorts of other chemicals can cause it to happen. Two such chemicals are 1) Paint and 2) Glue. It therefore becomes problematical to paint Lexan or to use self-adhesive decorative trim, for the plasticiser migrates within a short time-scale to produce super flexible paint and extremely brittle plastic. The next "shunt" that you have with your car will result in the body shell self-destructing, very much like smashing an electric light bulb. It is for this very reason that dire warnings are issued to the motor-bike fraternity to avoid paint or "stick ons" when using polycarbonate crash helmets, for failure to obey the rules renders the crash hat useless.

So where does that leave us? Well, there are specialist Lexan paints on the market whose chemical make-up overcomes this problem, and some of the water-based acrylics are also suitable. It will come as no surprise to find that specialist manufacturers within the model car profession market these specialist paints. Parma, from the States, and Tamiya from Japan, for instance, both offer "non embrittlement" paints with which to decorate their body shells. Usually such "Lexan paint" is specially formulated to work with its own thinner and therefore should not be used with other brands. Lexan paints may be brushed or sprayed but in general appear to be translucent when dry. Consequently an opaque base coat is usually beneficial.

Now, another major by-product of the Lexan body shell is that it is transparent, which has led to the widespread adoption of "painting on the inside". This technique, originating from the early days of slot car racing, offers two major advantages. With the paint on the inside of the shell, the viewer "sees" the colour through the high gloss, transparent plastic which means that one can get away with matt or semi matt paints and even poor paint application on the inside, for it still appears smooth and glossy from the outside. Furthermore, light abrasion of the outside of the body shell resulting from the inevitable collision with other cars or the track barrier will not in fact damage the paintwork.

These two advantages, however, are made less attractive by the difficulty many encounter by painting in reverse. Painting "backwards" is an acquired skill that comes with practice and can be mentally frustrating during the early attempts. Anyone with only a modicum of grey matter will have become used to working from the background forward as the prime route to the successful application of paint. Now we have the situation where the foreground comes first, followed in order by the mid-ground and background, the coat of opaque primer going on last. Muralling the bonnet of a Lexan car can be a bit fraught therefore! However, like most things, practice makes perfect and good paint jobs can result with just a little applied effort. Putting pin lines etc. on first is in fact very parallel to the requirements of pin lining on the "outside" as discussed earlier.

A useful by-product of the Lexan body shell is that panel lines, door outlines etc. are often moulded in "sunk" on the outside and "raised" on the inside of the body shell. A useful trick here is to paint the inside of the car and let it dry. Then with a sharp modelling blade, carefully scrape along these raised lines inside the body removing the paint from the top edge only of these raised lines. Overpainting these lines with a contrasting colour then allows the contrast to show through (only where the plastic was scraped clean) producing a neat parallel panel line.

Of course, all of the standard techniques of masking can still be used inside a Lexan shell provided that one remembers to do the whole thing in reverse.

Other areas within the definition of "Working Models" carry their own special problems. Fairground models, traction engines and live steam locomotives for instance. Fairground models, and for that matter narrow boats and other canal barges, present the rare example of subjects that are better brush painted than sprayed – an unusual statement, but in virtually every other case a sprayed finish will always be easier to achieve and will have a higher quality result. The main problem here is that the originals were invariably hand-painted, the lettering and decorative work being in many instances almost crude and amateur when compared to today's high-tech paint finishes.

In model form it is easy to mask and spray to produce perfect results that look somewhat artificial because of the conformity. Study of the prototype will reveal the errors brought about by hand finishing and these need to be incorporated in the model to produce the correct air of authenticity. That is not to say that one should be slapdash. On the contrary, this sort of careful brushwork requires just as much slow and painstaking work as the machine-painted model types. The very character of, say, a canal barge is epitomised in the manner in which the bargees hand-painted their decoration and any less effort on the part of the modeller to reproduce this effect in miniature will surely show up in the finished model.

To reproduce this work in small scales calls for a careful, steady hand and the smallest and finest of paint brushes.

Locomotives

Live steam, on the other hand, calls for yet a different approach. The prime additional worry here is that of heat, for the boiler on any steam-powered vehicle gets hot, really hot. Some paints don't like this at all and have been known to discolour at best, or at worst soften and bleed. The ideal solution for this type of problem is stove enamelling,

There is no doubt that lining adds to the appearance of this 3½in. gauge *Rob Roy* 0-6-0T built by Mr Wardropper of the S.M.E.E. (photo L. Lawrence).

but while this is possible in amateur environment it is far better done by a specialist, which in turn makes it difficult when many small parts are envisaged. Under amateur conditions, most live steam enthusiasts will etch-prime and brush-paint with oil-bound enamels. Precision Paints are by far the most commonly used brand, due to the fact that they have been formulated for just this very market, they can be bought in more sensible sized cans and, probably most important of all, they have been colour matched to almost every popular railway shade, not to mention road vehicles. On the debit side, of course, is the fact is that enamel paints take a long time to dry and require better attention to the environment in which they are used.

Furthermore, never lose sight of the fact that paints of this extended drying time (and this includes epoxides and urethanes) cause another problem if sprayed. The overspray – i.e. the paint in the atmosphere – lands wet and then dries where it lands, becoming difficult to remove later (this tends to get you in hot water if you spray indoors and the overspray dries on the furniture!). It is equally frustrating if other models are in the vicinity and wind up with a million paint spots on them that don't want to be removed. Remember to cover everything up (use damp newspaper) and this problem can be totally contained.

Despite the growing trend to spray paint, many still use a brush, which to me always seems like spoiling the ship for the proverbial ha'porth of tar. After all, if you've spent many months and much money on your 5½ foot locomotive, why make life difficult in the final stages?

Enamels lend themselves better to brush painting and provided all

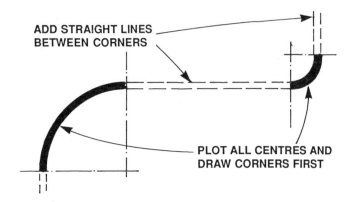

ADD STRAIGHT LINES BETWEEN CORNERS

PLOT ALL CENTRES AND DRAW CORNERS FIRST

of the preparatory steps have been correctly taken, brushed enamel finishes *can* be made to look "better than average".

Remember, as always, to choose the right shape and grade of brush and to smooth the paint out evenly. Working on cylindrical boilers is not easy, particularly if the boiler bands are already fitted. The general rule is to brush out along the boiler rather than round it. Having said that, however, it is not always practical. Often one can apply the paint along the boiler, brush it out around it, finishing with the very lightest of brushings out in the first direction. As with large models of aircraft, handling often becomes a problem and a hundredweight or so of locomotive is hardly the thing to suspend from a rusty nail in the ceiling. Always heed the "Wetline", the name given to the "edge" of the paint line. It is imperative that this wet edge is maintained so that the next paint-laden brush-stroke will flow and blend into the previously painted area. Failure to watch for this when painting larger models will cause a line to appear in the final surface where wet paint was laid alongside already drying paint. Keep this raw edge wet at all times, particularly where you "have to go round the other side" to continue painting, or be prepared to polish it out after the paint is fully dry – which consumes much time and elbow grease!!

Lining out models of this nature may be approached along traditional lines, using careful freehand with a proper lining brush, or by using draughtsman's pens charged with thin paint.

These methods call for a steady hand and careful planning. Fixing the subject in place and creating a raised, adjacent area, say from a pile of books or from scrap wood, will allow the hand to rest on this firm surface at such an angle as to be comfortable. Discomfort while handling the brush or pen will only lead to extra effort, resulting usually in poor work. Pre-planning of the lines is an essential move and the use of a rule and compasses is a must! Carefully plot the centres of all

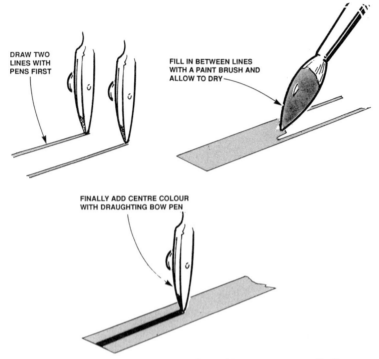

DRAW TWO
LINES WITH
PENS FIRST

FILL IN BETWEEN LINES
WITH A PAINT BRUSH AND
ALLOW TO DRY

FINALLY ADD CENTRE COLOUR
WITH DRAUGHTING BOW PEN

radii and cover with small patches of masking tape – usually three or four layers thick – to give somewhere for the point of the compasses to rest upon so as not to (a) skid across the shiny paint surface and (b) not to make a "point mark" in the paintwork. As in the base coat, it pays to keep the wet line if at all possible, and the straight line pen work used to join up the radiused corners really needs adding while the corners are still wet. Many prefer to use artists' inks to carry out this type of lining exercise, which is quite acceptable provided that it is remembered that an outer coat of lacquer is required to "seal in" the surface detail. As mentioned before, it will pay dividends to keep to a common brand of materials for both base coats and surface lacquers; be warned, however, that many clear lacquers yellow badly with age and/or heat and may well cause a major colour change. If in doubt, it is best to consult with the paint manufacturer before taking any risks. Remember that boiler temperatures may be anything up to 170-180°C and tell the paint people.

Trim Lines Like all model painting, multiple trim lines can benefit enormously by the use of carefully prepared stencils or masks. As an example, consider the case of a traction engine wheel with a pin line around the rim and decorative lines on each spoke. Assuming that precision is required rather than the freehand approach (this of course is entirely a matter of taste) the rim line can be obtained by creating a false "centre" to the hub and using, once more, the draughtsman's compasses. Multiple rings and multiple colours can all be done before removing the "centre".

The spokes provide yet another example of how to cheat and can be made all the same by the fabrication of a simple cardboard (or even shim metal or plastic) mask. The mask should have one curved end to fit inside the wheel rim and the other curved to fit around the wheel hub. Locating tabs or slots can be cut in the mask to enable it to be lined up accurately with each spoke in turn as the mask is rotated round the wheel. The shape of the design on the spoke can now be cut out and used as a guide to the draughting pen, paint-brush or air-brush. Using rapid drying paints or inks will enable the mask to be rotated from spoke to spoke quite quickly, and, of course, each spoke decoration will not only be identical but properly spaced in relation to the edges of the spoke.

'REVERSE' PINSTRIPES AND MULTIPLES

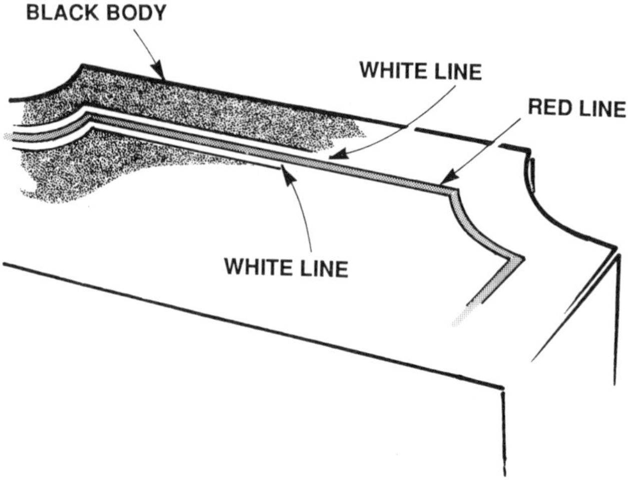

BLACK BODY

WHITE LINE

RED LINE

WHITE LINE

STAGE 1 - SPRAY TENDER WITH INNER LINE COLOUR FIRST (RED?)
STAGE 2 - APPLY 1/32 IN. TAPE (EXACT WIDTH OF TAPE DEPENDS ON SCALE) WHERE INNER LINE IS TO GO
STAGE 3 - SPRAY OUTER LINE COLOUR ALL OVER (WHITE)
STAGE 4 - APPLY 5/32 IN. TAPE OVER THE TOP OF THE EXISTING TAPE (MAKE SURE IT IS CENTRAL)
STAGE 5 - SPRAY BLACK
STAGE 6 - REMOVE TAPE

All this traditional approach can, however, be overtaken by modern mask and spray techniques and as we have seen before, tackling the job in reverse using the high accuracy masking tapes made for the printed circuit business enables highly accurate, multi-colour lining to be achieved easier than you can say "airbrush"!

Consider, as a hypothetical example, a black locomotive with a white/red/white pin line system. Let us say that the width of each pin line is 40 thou. First, a trip to the local graphic art shop to obtain two reels of tape, one at 40 thou wide and one at 120 thou. Now lightly spray the area of the loco where the red stripe will ultimately be with red paint and let it cure thoroughly. With the 40 thou tape and a sharp scalpel, lay down the tape wherever the line is required. Carefully trim the edges and joins and ensure that curved corners are, in fact, round and not egg shaped. When satisfied with the taping, spray over the tape with white and allow that to dry.

Phase two now, with the application of the 120 thou tape on top of the 40 thou tape that is already there. Take special care to get this wide tape exactly astride the existing tape and equally spaced each side. This is particularly important at the corners and the radii. Remember that there is no paint at risk just yet so take your time and if it is not quite right, lift the wide tape and reposition until you are completely satisfied. Now, and only now, is the time to shoot on a good, all over coat of black (remembering the golden rule that two light coats are always better than one heavy coat). Now lift off and peel back the double layer of tape (both the wide and the narrow!) and, wonder of

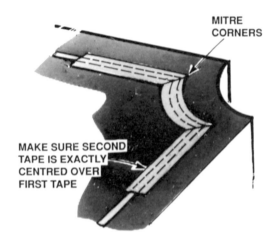

MITRE CORNERS

MAKE SURE SECOND TAPE IS EXACTLY CENTRED OVER FIRST TAPE

wonders, the white/red/white pin stripes appear as if by magic. Top marks for lateral thought!

Lettering and company logos are often obtainable in one or other of the transfer or rub-down products especially produced for models of this sort, but if they are not then the home-made variety can be produced (as detailed earlier) and applied as normal. Alternatively a steady hand with pen and/or brush can yield excellent results. Remember the fact that such lettering and badges are much better done "off the model" if at all possible, but if not, then consider the masking film and airbrush route that must surely give the most professional results. Multiple cut film or liquid masks will enable the most complex designs to be achieved "one piece at a time". Of course this method, as with home-made transfers or hand painting, does pre-suppose that you know what is supposed to be there in the first place! Although this, at face value, seems a stupid statement, many modellers spoil the finished product by producing, say, excellent letters but to an incorrect type, style or letter spacing. Never guess this – always work from an authenticated reference work – then capitalise upon the High Street photocopy shops.

Copy the lettering or logo, enlarging or reducing during the copying until the correct size is obtained. Use the finished photocopy to make stencils, masks etc. or to transfer onto film or liquid masks prior to cutting. A useful tip is to take a sheet of matt masking film with you to the copiers and have the final size lettering copied directly onto the film. Applying the film, then, to the model and cutting out in situ offers the best possible route to success!

8　　SMALLER SCALES

Working in the Smaller Scale

When dropping down from the larger sizes of working models some of the problems disappear and others are created. In general it is still a valid argument that a sprayed finish will usually produce a better result than that applied by paint-brush. However, things are never that simple and the very small sizes of, say, 1/72nd scale aircraft, OO gauge model railways or 25mm military figures demand the utmost finesse whether sprayed *or* brushed.

Much of the subject of pre-preparation still holds good: metal models will still benefit from etch primers and an all-over coat of grey primer is still valid on plastic/wood mixed construction models. However, it is here that one starts to fall foul of some of the myths, mixed with fact, that surround the hobby.

Let us take a look at the small scale plastic kit first and consider some of the problems.

First of all they are made from rigid, injection moulded styrene. Now styrene dissolves in many solvents and many of these solvents are employed by the followers of the plastic side of our hobby to stick the parts together. In fact they do not "stick" in the fine sense of the word, but fuse or weld the parts together by virtue of the fact that the solvents soften the edges of the plastic causing them actually to melt together as in the welding of metal, although no heat is used here, purely chemical dissolution. Consequently it is logical to accept that the use of some solvent-based paints would have the same melting effect and cause total ruination of the model. To this end, the entire industry has been built on the use of the ½oz. tinlets and jars of enamel in a multitude of authentically matched hues that cover virtually every aspect of the plastic kit builder's requirement.

This, however, is the cause of other problems. The main cause for concern is the fact that the matt enamels (used in the main for military aircraft and vehicles) dry quite quickly and it may well become difficult to hide the brush marks. Coupled with this is the fact that such paints are easily softened by the thinner used, which then tends to be a problem when applying contrasting colours on top of existing colours. To this end one must learn to work quickly and evenly when applying the second colour, endeavouring to cover in one pass and avoiding "going back over" too often to brush out the colour. Such softening, often leading to colour change by intermixing, is also particularly prevalent when using metallic colours such as gold, silver and copper, all of which are used widely for small detail work on such models.

Of course, this is not a new problem. It happens if one applies matt colour dopes to working model aircraft for much the same reason and can be reduced to an acceptable level by careful brushwork or eliminated altogether by spraying.

Now despite the solvent problem, many non-enamel paints can still be used, providing that you know what you are doing. Ladling on coloured cellulose with a paint-brush will lead to disaster, yet applied carefully by airbrushing, cellulose has much to offer.

Plastic Models

Initially, the preparation of a plastic model may well feature areas that have to be filled or built up with proprietary body putties. In later stages, where major conversion work is undertaken, other materials may well be used, perhaps other types of plastics or even balsa wood. Either way, the model's surface will not be the same all over, a fact that will almost certainly show when the thin, thin coats of paint are applied. Remember here too (or maybe here even more so!) too thick a coat of paint will virtually obliterate much of the finely etched surface detail that has become the trademark of the toolmaker's art in this hobby area. Consequently some degree of "levelling" is needed and many would resort to a good coat of matt grey enamel as this base colour. Others would follow the cellulose route, for a *light* mist coat of cellulose car primer not only produces this homogeneous surface finish, but, in many instances, also provides a substantial key, the primer microscopically etching into the plastic. Subsequent colour coats can either be brushed on (using enamels) or if desired, can be sprayed, sticking to cellulose throughout. Provided that light mist coats are applied, cellulose has much to offer in many areas. White, for example, is not an easy colour with which to work. White enamels go yellow with age; so for that matter do many of the clear varnishes used to finish a model in gloss or semi gloss. Furthermore brushmarks show up badly in white. Silver is another problem colour, difficult to apply evenly by brush, and whether enamel or cellulose, for the enamels tend to age quickly.

So if, for argument's sake, you are into assembling plastic kits of airliners, you could have a handful of bother. Both white and silver cel-

1/100th scale plastic kits. F4 is brush painted, F105 is airbrushed. Note inability to duplicate "soft" edge shading when using a brush. Many experts would say that the soft edge spraying on models of this small size is grossly over scale, yet somehow it still manages the illusion of looking right!

lulose spray easily and I have examples of early plastic kits – some in excess of 20 years old – that show no sign of ageing! However, do heed the warning and don't try brush-painting cellulose onto your brand new Airfix kit.

Many acrylics are also of use with these plastics and very often local garages will provide the odd eggcup-full of motor car colours if simply asked politely. If you buy them, there is the rub that cellulose and acrylics don't come in ½oz. tins and jars as stated earlier, though if you are a serious modeller or if you model as part of a like-minded group, the investment in terms of a ½ litre of cellulose, colour matched as described earlier, is definitely worthwhile.

Now reverting to the base plastic for a minute, there is styrene and there is styrene. Some manufacturers of plastic kits have for some while been using a cheaper form of plastic. Whether this is reconstituted waste or just a cheaper formulation is something of which I am not sure. What I *do* know for certain is that adhesion of non-enamel product is suspect! Despite tests which show conclusively that the solvents *do* attack the surface and that keying does take place, it is quite easy to remove the colour coat and the primer beneath, often when removing the masking tape/film between colours. Despite all queries as to why and many tests, no real solution has ever been put forward.

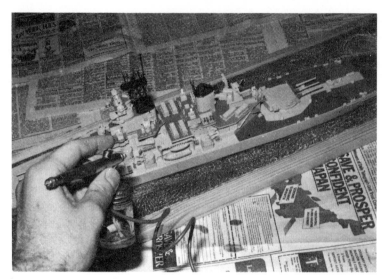

A spray gun or even a fine airbrush have limited use on very detailed small models, except for initial undercoating, a final coat of matt varnish or an all-over weathering coat. Masking on tiny models is difficult and there is little point in using hand-painted liquid mask.

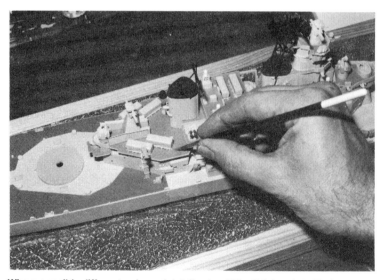

Where possible different-coloured details should be finish-painted before cementing in position, which is the only way to get sharp, straight joint lines. Where details are moulded in with the main moulding, extreme care should be taken to get a neat line with the minimum of paint.

Fortunately help is to hand from the automotive industry. Yes, we're back to the two-pack, acid cured etch primers that will work equally well on metal *and* plastics. Most plastics, that is; it will still pay the enthusiast to ask diligently of the supplier or solicit a small sample to try out. As previously mentioned, many of these primers are of the high-build type, predominantly as an aid to filling holes and scratches on cars, and therefore should not be applied with a heavy hand for they will build thickness quickly and obliterate surface detail. On the other hand, of course, when applied over other materials within the realms of kit adaptation this high-build property can be to our advantage!

Most of these primers are of the rapid drying variety and really are not at home with brush-painting, so that the use of an airbrush becomes almost a necessity. Remember to clean out the airbrush thoroughly (and quickly!) to remove any traces of the acid catalyst from within the jet/needle assembly.

Once primered and base coated, the final finishing technique is as already described. The use of tape, film, liquid or sometimes even cut paper masks is paramount in producing the required end result. Careful colour matching is important and sometimes even grossly "overscale" painting can be devastatingly effective.

There are many that would argue that such overscale effects spoil rather than enhance the finished model, yet I, for one, have seen repeated examples of the "illusion" triumphing over the "realistic".

My own interest in the plastic kit theatre is models to 1/100 scale (a rare breed, getting more rare with the passage of time). Now assuming that the overspray on the real Spitfire, Phantom, etc., etc. is in the order of ½ inch or so, to the scale of one hundredth, this would represent one two hundredth of an inch or about 5 or 6 thou. It is virtually impossible to achieve this degree of overspray, even with the high quality artists' airbrushes, when used freehand and it cannot sensibly be achieved with masks or stippled with a paint brush. Probably the most accurate representation of this foggy edge in this small scale would be a hard edge, for only with a magnifying glass could the viewer see the edge if scale overspray *could* be achieved. Despite all of this, overscale soft edges achieved by careful freehand spraying often appear to be right in the eye of the viewer even when we all really know that they are not.

The proof of the pudding, of course, is when the two different approaches come up against each other in the competitive world. If judged by experts, the hard edged paint job will usually win, but if judged by the viewing modellers, as is so often the case at such events, the airbrushed feather-edge will win hands down. Another

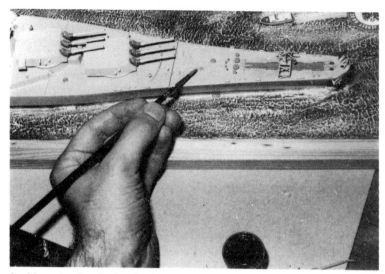

Avoid overloading the brush when touching in small details – it is easy to add a little more paint but a lengthy and tedious job to clean up a surplus. Always rest the brush hand on something firm and fixed.

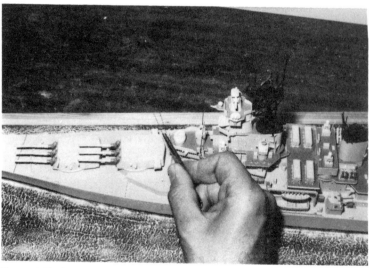

The modeller is here attaching a whip aerial after completing painting of the deck and fixed details. The clearer the field the better the paint job will be, so anything which can be left off till after painting should be!

area where this type of overscale treatment can be seen with considerable effect is the military vehicles and dioramas produced by Francois Verlinden. Here too it is a bone of contention whether it is too much "over the top" with many critics to be found. Yet there are many more who would give their eye teeth to be able to paint like that!

Model Railways

Not only aircraft and military vehicles but the model railway scene too falls foul of the crude application of paint. Again the usual choice of material is the now almost obligatory small jar or tin of enamel. While it could be argued that many railway wagons, lineside buildings etc. are of matt finish, many are glossy with the attendant problems of drying times. Remember when working with gloss enamels and a paintbrush that scrupulous cleanliness and the highest quality paints and brushes are essential to a good result. Retaining a wet line, rapid and smooth brush strokes and careful mixing and preparation of the paint are all areas which cannot be skimped on in time or money. In these small scales it is often not possible to rub down or cut back and polish paint surfaces to remove errors and blemishes, and therefore it is even more important to get it right first time. With model railways it is not uncommon to be working with metal and/or plastic and sometimes both in the same model. Remember the new automotive primers and capitalise upon their advantages. Once more, spray for preference and keep brush application to the minor detail. If you are serious about model railway work, you too will follow the plastic kit techniques and consider the use of cellulose and acrylic paints even if you do need to bulk buy. White is the same problem for a carriage roof as it is for that of an airliner and previous comments apply.

Weathering

Some railway modellers produce pristine models, others (as with other aspects of the great modelling hobby) prefer to see the models in their "working dirt". Dirtying up a model, or "weathering" as it is commonly called, is a matter of taste. I like it – many don't. If you do, then apply the dirt and grime with care. Every prototype has its own characteristic and dirt on one vehicle won't necessarily collect in the same place as on a different vehicle. Furthermore consider carefully the "colour" of dirt. Soot is usually black and can be seen on both steam and diesel locomotives and as cordite stains around the gun apertures on some aircraft. Oil is usually *not* black but dark brown and if oil leaks are reasonably recent then they will usually be glossy to simulate wet oil. Other stains, limescale for instance, will be other colours, rust on the hulls of steel boats and ships will be shades of red, while corrosion on aluminium wagons, aircraft etc. is, more often than not, off-white or pale grey.

It becomes just as necessary to study the colour and placement of such blemishes as it was to study the "real thing" to get the base colour and markings correct. Once again, weathering can be lightly done to a scale level or can be overdone to suit individual taste. Whether clean or dirty stock is decided upon, scenery, in either a model railway situation or in dioramas to back up a plastic kit or two, usually *is* dirty. One rarely sees a building as new and grass, trees, fences etc. are all going to be dull and *never* of one consistent colour. Careful use of a paint-brush to provide dulling down is not at all difficult, the main drawback being that of knowing when to stop. Much of this colouring technique, whether it be shading of exhaust stains on a Spitfire or dirtying up the front edges of railway wagons, can be achieved using the "dry brush" method. Here the brush is dipped into the paint of suitable hue and then as much of the paint as possible is removed by wiping the brush on the edge of the can. Now remove still more paint on a cloth or tissue until the brush is almost completely dry. Only at this stage do you attack the model, depositing this almost dry paint onto the relevant areas. This dry brushing applies minuscule amounts of paint and being virtually dry, there is no real wet edge to spoil the effect.

Like many aspects of painting, the best weathering is applied by spraying. With care, dirty colour can be dusted along the various edges of a chosen vehicle to the extent that the dirt builds up in the various corners and crevices as it does on the real thing.

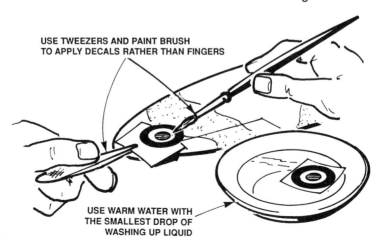

USE TWEEZERS AND PAINT BRUSH
TO APPLY DECALS RATHER THAN FINGERS

USE WARM WATER WITH
THE SMALLEST DROP OF
WASHING UP LIQUID

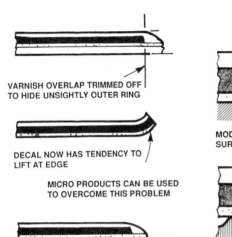

VARNISH OVERLAP TRIMMED OFF
TO HIDE UNSIGHTLY OUTER RING

DECAL NOW HAS TENDENCY TO
LIFT AT EDGE

MICRO PRODUCTS CAN BE USED
TO OVERCOME THIS PROBLEM

DECAL AS SUPPLIED

FEATHERED EDGE TO VARNISH
OVERLAP GIVES BETTER ADHESION
BUT 'EDGE' SHOWS!

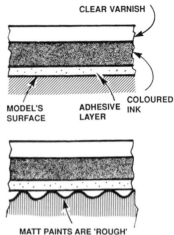

CLEAR VARNISH

MODEL'S SURFACE   ADHESIVE LAYER   COLOURED INK

MATT PAINTS ARE 'ROUGH'
MAKING ADHESION POOR

With smaller scales such as these, a great deal more emphasis is placed on the use of transfers, whether of the waterslide type or those applied with methylated spirit, rather than hand painting insignia and markings. Many kits of parts come with such transfers but equally there are many specialist suppliers that produce excellent products to meet these requirements. The application of such transfers is not difficult and is usually adequately covered in the accompanying instructions.

However, there can still be "tricks of the trade" that can be used to produce a more professional finish. Waterslide transfers or decals are not easily applied over anything other than a smooth gloss surface, as they don't adhere too well to some matt paints and don't pull down properly over, say, a row of rivets. Specialist product lines such as Micro system can help enormously. Microsol, Microset, Microgloss, etc. are all products that can help. Gloss coat can be applied to the area where the transfer is to be fixed first to improve adhesion. Microset and Microsol can be used to improve adhesion and to soften the transfer to enable it to conform to uneven or irregular surfaces. Mattcoat can be applied over the transfer to bring it down to the level of the matt paint (many plastic kit transfers are glossy when in fact they should be matt but the reverse is just as true!). In many cases it will pay to give the entire model a final surface of clear varnish – right over any transfers – to bring everything down to a common level, be it gloss, matt or eggshell.

Even here it is necessary to be a bit careful, and remember to do some homework. Gloss clear enamels yellow with age, as has already been stated, and if at all possible, acrylic clear lacquers, sprayed on, are to be preferred. Matt clear should not be applied over transparencies – cockpit canopies etc. *are* gloss and polished. Similarly, gloss clear needs keeping off of tyres (except for pristine showroom condition models). Military dioramas often require a mix of matt and gloss finishes. Camouflage on tanks for instance is more customarily matt, but if the tank is battling its way through muddy fields, the mud will be glossy if it is supposed to be wet and that includes the mud dripping from the body edges, wheels, tracks etc.

Figures

Tanks are, of course, part of the vast military modelling scene. There is a whole army of modellers whose interest is in the military figure, either as a subject in its own right or in conjunction with military vehicles. Books have been written on all the aspects of such modelling and cover the originals right through to how to amend and adapt figures from one stance to another or even how to make them from scratch. From our point of view, they still need to be painted and apart from primers and all-over colours, this is an area where the paintbrush reigns supreme and the airbrush has yet to gain serious recognition. Once again the need for careful preparation is important and all of the points already covered apply here as well. On metal or plastic figures an all-over coat of etch primer (two-pack) is ideal although as little, if any, masking is done with this type of painting, plain grey primer or light grey or white matt enamel works almost as well. In general most good military figures will be metal or rigid plastic. Some, however, are of a soft, flexible plastic of the polythene type. None of the oil or cellulose-based colours will adhere properly to this type of plastic and it is best to use only the plastic water-based acrylic paints most often encountered in artists' shops. However, if such a figure is primed with one or, better, two thin coats of thinned-out PVA glue, conventional enamels can be used.

As we have seen with the high quality plastic kit, the degree of surface detail in most military figures is amazing and heavy-handedness with the primer can all but obscure this detail. At the same time, high-build primers can be used with care to build up those areas where adaptations and modifications have been made or even to create folds in clothing, uniforms, boots etc.

For the majority of figure work small tinlets of enamels (matt, gloss and metallics) are quite sufficient although most serious students of this art will quickly move on. Two main areas seem to solicit regular support – artists' oils and acrylics. Most of the acrylics are of the modern "poster paint" family and are water soluble, making thinning them quite easy. Application is simple but some care needs taking with brushmarking. Some specialist acrylics are somewhat on the thick side, making them particularly suited to gap filling or the building up of the surface for detail (as with high-build primers) when used straight from the can or tube. Considerable thinning is needed to produce a viscosity suited to smooth brushwork. Most of these types of acrylic, whilst water soluble in the liquid state, dry to a waterproof finish (essential to avoid the next colour from softening the existing colour). It is imperative, therefore, that brushes and spray equipment are rapidly and thoroughly cleaned out, for once the paint has gone hard it is difficult to remove and will permanently damage both the brush and the wallet (see chapter on brushes – price thereof!). These thick acrylics can be worked with a stippling brush to produce textured finishes, or can be peaked, but due to the rapid drying time it is best to keep this to small areas at a time. Most of these thicker varieties tend to dry matt, but many of the more runny versions dry to an eggshell sheen.

It is not uncommon to find that some artists' acrylics are not completely opaque and this may be used to advantage when applying dark over light colours, producing quite pleasing effects on, say, models of horses. Most paints from the art store can be used successfully in figure painting but there can be no doubt that some of the best examples in the field have been executed in artists' oils. It is considered by many that such oils offer a richness in colour and texture unmatched by other finishes.

Oil paints, like brushes, vary enormously from brand to brand and in general the superior quality artists' oils will be among the more expensive. It may well be best to attempt to work with this quality rather than go off at half cock using students' oils.

One of the better aspects of working in oils is the simplicity of mixing small quantities of special colour. Oil paints can be used straight from the tube, simply squeezing out a small quantity onto a clean palette and pulling the brush through the paint to load it. Mixing on this palette can be achieved as the artist would do it and reference to library books on oil painting for beginners (even if they are painting flat pictures!) will yield much information on the shades that can be mixed and the colours with which to mix them.

Oils, like most paints, benefit from *not* being applied in one thick coat but several thin ones. Too much paint too quickly can eliminate fine detail and can cause brush-marks to show. However, as always there are exceptions to prove every rule and oils in the experienced hand may be used to build up surface detail and texture. The slower drying of oil colours allows the careful blending of colours in situ, a particularly useful property when working in shades of flesh or in certain clothing colours and finishes, leather tunics for example.

Specialised thinners and cleaning agents are needed with oil paints, although cellulose thinner or white spirit will clean the brushes. Neither of these solvents is suitable for thinning, however, and if turps is to be used it should be real distilled turpentine and *not* the white spirit-based materials known as "turps substitute".

Only small quantities of distilled turps should be used, for too much may well produce the same problem as cellulose and matt enamels, where the base coat can soften to the extent that it may even blend with the top colour. Experienced figure painters can benefit from this characteristic to produce blended colours for faces and uniforms, but the novice might do well to avoid such delicate techniques until a little experience has been accrued. A by-product of using distilled turps can also be capitalised upon, and this is the fact that its addition to the oils tends to remove some of the gloss. Linseed oil or Copal oil are other common additives (linseed of course being the prime constituent) that can be used by the modeller. Adding linseed tends to slow the drying and increase the gloss while copal tends to increase the speed of drying. (See Chapter 1.)

Where there is a major difference between figures and other forms of model painting is that with models of vehicles, the prototype is inevitably painted. Therefore the model is painted too. With military figures, the "real thing" is flesh and blood and the uniform is usually fabric with the possibility of unpainted metal inclusions. Consequently there is much more artistic requirement in figure painting and less technical expertise, and this is what makes military figure modelling so different from other branches of our hobby. Artistically one needs to know where the light and dark shades occur. In a face, for instance, upper cheeks, forehead, chin and the area above the upper lip are highlight areas whilst hairline, inner edge of eyes and sides of nose, under lower lip and under the chin are the lowlights.

After applying the base face colour, darker tones can be brushed onto and blended into the creases. Highlights can be similarly added and, due to the slower drying nature of oil paints, brushing through, often with a change of the direction of the paint-brush, is used to provide changes of blended shades. Dry brush techniques discussed earlier are also valid and a dry brush lightly brushed over the figure will pick out only the raised detail. "Peaking", a technique of using a pointed brush to raise small points in still wet thick paint, enables the modeller to produce raised detail such as would be found on fur clothes. Like all forms of modelling, careful research into uniforms is just as essential as research into colours and markings of, say, a Spitfire, for only when this information is fully to hand can a modeller even start to capture the character of the original in miniature.

9 OTHER ASPECTS

Spin Offs and Alternatives

Model making is an old established hobby and one where the requirement to paint has always been with us. Few of us dabble in every branch of this hobby, yet, amazingly, many of us pursue more than one aspect, even if one takes priority and the others are secondary.

With painting, too, many of us have alternative interests associated with, if not directly related to, our prime model interest. There are those of us who paint (or repaint) the kiddies' toys, dabble in oils, or even (more mundane) paint the bedroom walls. Sidelines to the main route of one's hobby can often be just as satisfying as the main stream.

Painting figures with oils for instance is not far removed from "proper" painting on canvas, which in its turn is not far removed from one of today's major sources of "pop" art – decorated tee and sweat shirts.

Fabric Paints Now one of the major aspects of model building is the fact that *your* model is unique and differs from all of the others out of the same mould. Individual skills, interests, and technique see to that. However, the mass produced slogan upon a shirt makes one the same as thousands of others, so why not paint your own and be as individual as your model? The skills and techniques are no different from painting models, only the materials involved change. Fabric paints (or dyes to be absolutely accurate) have been around for years and are available from most art and craft shops. They are usually fairly thick in consistency and can be applied by brush straight from the jar. The end result is as good as your imagination and slogans and pictures backing up your own model interest are not at all difficult to achieve. For the lady of the house, the technique can carry over into quite intricate decorative work on, say, the corners of pillowcases or table-cloths, offering not only an extension to an existing hobby but often producing a family involvement that might otherwise not exist. More recently fabric dyes have come onto the market that are of such a consistency that they can be airbrushed, bringing yet another modelling technique to bear. Airtex by Badger is just one such example of these dyes.

In general these dyes need to be "fixed" after a painting or decoration is complete and the most usual requirement here is to cover the design with a clean sheet of brown paper and iron over the paper (and the pattern) with a domestic iron set to as hot a temperature as the fabric will stand. This heat treatment effectively cures the dye, making it permanent.

Now there is permanent and permanent. Most dye manufacturers advise that, once cured, their products are machine washable. Some are and some are not. Colours can fade quickly if machine washed too hot or too often and, if it is possible, it is usually better to try to avoid letting the garment or fabric become too dirty and restrict washing to that done by hand.

Pop Art Custom painting is another area that has grown to represent a sort of classic "pop" art of the generation. Many are the shows for custom cars and bikes and many are the magazines catering for them.

Custom painting is, more often than not, sprayed, but there *are* excellent examples to be seen of brushwork. The hobby has spawned its own supporting industry (as, of course, has model making) whereby all manner of add-on goodies can now be obtained. From the painting point of view a whole new range of acrylic based paints have appeared on the market, many of which can be incorporated into models in exactly the same manner as with the full-size.

Peacock motif associated with the author on the bonnet (hood) of his car. Patient masking and a simple airbrush are the main requirements.

The mainstay of custom paints are single-pack acrylics which go under such exotic names as "Candy Apple" and similar. Candies are not at all difficult to use but do require their own special thinner. Probably the greatest difference to be found in candies when compared with other modelling paints is the fact that they are translucent. This is a double-edged sword for, from the advantage point of view, candies need a base coat. From the disadvantage point, their translucency means that a very *even* coating is required, otherwise brushmarks or even spray patterns can show. In fact, re-coating with candies must be even and all over, for each coat progressively darkens the translucent colour.

Once you have accepted this problem and learnt to apply the paint evenly the base coat advantage may be considered, for the translucent top coat relies heavily on its undercoat. Many swear by white as the best undercoat, allowing the best reflectivity through the translucent candy and creating a feeling of depth unparalleled in any other paint. Yet one is not restricted in this choice, for silver, gold and even black base colours produce not only startling effects but colours that appear totally different from each other, even though the top coat is common. This change opens up a whole new approach to fancy paintwork on the non-scale subject where the very sky is the limit. Subtlety is the name of the game and using, say, a white base coat with gold patterns *beneath* a candy top coat will result in a coloured model with subtle but different shades of trim where it goes over the gold patterning. Candies are available in a wide range of colours, are easy to apply (given the conditions already mentioned) and will polish to a very high gloss. Clear acrylics from the same family can be used as a multiple layer overcoat to "seal in" any fine patterning work.

Other paints from within the "custom" families carry equally exotic names, such as Eeriedess, Vreeble, Flip-flop and Metalflake.

Eeriedess has many properties similar to the oils used for figure painting inasmuch as they can be peaked or combed or even patted with crumpled kitchen foil to form a pattern within the paint surface, lacquering over to seal in once the main coat is dry. Vreeble, on the other hand, dries so quickly that it contracts and cracks up, leaving a crazy paving appearance where the base coat (usually silver or gold) shows through. Once again clear lacquer is applied all over as a sealer. Flip-flop is perhaps one of the more exciting special paints that in use will completely transform even a mediocre paint job. Like Candies, Flip-flop is a translucent colour – only more so. It also has most peculiar reflective properties such that depending upon how the light falls upon it may appear to change colour, or even disappear from

Fish-scale effect achieved by simple mask moved along in stages. Demonstrated is how to remove masking tapes – *always* pull tape back on itself – *never* at 90° to surface. Pull gently and consistently to ensure a clean edge. Cellulose paints may be left to dry before removing tapes. Hard cure paints such as epoxides benefit from having the tape removed before the resins have fully cured. Ordinary crepe paper tape used here, 1/16″ wide for the pin line and 1″ wide for the remainder. P.V.C. tapes are better for epoxy paints.

view altogether. It might seem like an April Fool's joke but it really does behave exactly like that. Used on models of racing cars it can cause great concern to the viewer as the model will appear to change colour as it goes round corners.

Probably the most spectacular of all of the "special" custom paints is known as Metalflake. As its name suggests, Metalflake is just that, small flakes of highly polished metal contained within a lacquer carrying base. 'Flake is supplied dry, in tubs, much like the "glitter" that one might buy at Christmastime. It is most usually mixed with clear lacquer and sprayed on, but if you wish to try it, use one of the simpler mini-guns such as the Badger 250 or the small Revell spraygun and avoid the use of expensive, high finesse airbrushes.

The sheer brightness of the flake is what makes it stand out visually, the physical size of the particles of flake are such that when dry it takes on the appearance of very coarse glasspaper, requiring several coats of clear lacquer over it to produce a smooth surface. Of course, like most custom painting the end result is only as good as one's imagination. 'Flake comes in a wide range of colours in its own right, but it doesn't stop there, for 'flake can be contained in colours or coloured over. Because of the transparent nature of Candies, there is no end to the permutations that can be worked with 'flake.

Opalescent One final custom paint that is quite widely used on the model front is Pearlescent finish. This is similar to (but much more subtle than) the metallics which have been common in both enamels and cellulose for many years. Pearl paints are usually of quite subtle hue with just a hint of metallic causing the result to look rather like mother-of-pearl. They make an excellent base coat for fancy custom work and English modellers will have seen my car around the model shows over the last few years. This has a "snow pearl" base, with silver flake side panels. Trim is in deep red pin stripes, with fogged edging, to match the upholstery and the bonnet encompasses the now traditional peacock. The "go-faster" style lettering on each side of the car was carried out with a cheap airbrush and a cut paper stencil. No-one can claim that I don't practise what I preach!

Allowing modelling enthusiasm to spill over into other areas is no bad thing, for it opens the eyes to other aspects of painting, for example, that will reflect in more skills and greater knowledge which in turn will reflect in an increasing standard of modelling.

Not only that but the refurbishing of kiddies' bikes, pedal cars and other toys is an enjoyable exercise in cost saving (allowing more to be spent on modelling perhaps!). In terms of finances, the modelling hobby is not a cheap one – what hobby is? Any sideline that earns a pound or two is not to be dismissed lightly. Moving up in size from custom painting a 1/12th or 1/8th scale model car to decorating the petrol tank of the bike belonging to next door's teenage son is no big deal. Such a project can be undertaken with existing modelling paints and existing modelling tools. It will earn you a bit and at the same time allow you full rein of the imagination, increasing your skills as you go. However, if bikes are involved take due regard to earlier comment concerning the use of paint and stickers on polycarbonates. If you *do* want to paint a crash helmet make absolutely certain that it is G.R.P. and not polycarbonate.

One should never lose sight of the fact that painting is an industry in its own right and that we, as modellers, use only a fraction of it. Airbrushes, for example have been around since before the turn of the century and are used by the thousand in other industries. We seem to have only discovered them recently and are often so busy following our own chosen route that we become blinkered to what others are doing. Make time to go out and talk to others. Watch artists at work. See what sort of paints are available outside of modelling. Study other uses of tools – all of which will result in a wealth of new knowledge, a better understanding and an increase in skills and interests.

APPENDIX 1

VARNISH COMPATIBILITY
Table of basic types of model finish

Types	Manufacturer	Remarks
Polyurethanes; Matt Gloss Satin	Ronseal,* Kingston Diamond,* Translac,* Humbrol,* Coverite,* Crown* etc.	Gives superb overall finish over enamels, dopes, decals etc. Does not need to be sprayed due to excellent covering characteristics. Also used as fuel proofer for flying model aircraft.
Varnishes: Matt Gloss	Humbrol, Joy, also Fuel Proofers etc.	Not quite as good a finish as one might quite expect, useful though for attaching fine parts or filling fine joints. Also used as fuel proofer for flying model aircraft.
Lacquer: Matt Gloss	Frisk Lac*	Mostly Aerosol. Gives excellent flat finish on plastic aircraft and tanks and gloss on large-scale cars (and can also be used over enamels and decals).
Spray varnishes:	Microscale: (USA)* (A) Dullcote/Glosscote*	Only to be applied by airbrush, assists decal finishing. Can be used over enamels and decals or plastic models.

*Use mask when applying by spray.

APPENDIX 2

PAINTING AND DECAL APPLICATION TROUBLE SHOOTING CHART

Decal problem	Cause and remedy
Decals lift away from model surface whilst drying.	Prolonged soaking has diluted adhesive solution or decal has been applied to a matt surface. Remove decal and coat model with gloss varnish.
Decal splits when dampened or applied to model.	Probably decal sheet is aged and can be saved by spraying the decal sheet with varnish before cutting up and re-wetting. If decal splits on model it has to be scrapped.
Bubbles appear under decal even after pressing down with blotter.	Prick bubbles with pin, apply water and press down again. If decals continue to bubble or lift up mix *PVA adhesive* with water apply by brush under decal and press down. When dry, excess glue can be removed with a damp cloth.
Carrier film visible after decal has dried.	Decal was not trimmed prior to application and a matt surface has revealed the carrier film which appears reflective under certain light. Careful hand painting with the background colour thus removing the carrier film, to be considered prior to final finish.
Decal once applied and dried later found to be in the wrong position.	Insufficient research during finishing. May be removed by pressing Sellotape on it and pulling away or soaking in warm water. If varnishing has taken place, complete removal along with the paint has to be considered using *Brake Fluid*.
Letraset decal splits or cracks on application.	Vigorous rubbing down has shattered decal or backing sheet has slipped during the operation. Remove with Sellotape.
Wrinkles occur on surface or edges lift up of Letraset decal.	Not burnished down enough, apply backing paper and re-burnish.
Once positioned, Letraset decal later found to be incorrectly placed.	Can only be removed by pressing Sellotape on marking and pulling up. Regrettably it cannot be salvaged.

Painting problem	Cause and remedy
Brushes shed hairs during painting.	Cheap brushes – throw them away and save up for some better quality ones. If hairs have been applied to the model leave the paint to dry, remove the hair with tweezers – sand smooth with wet and dry paper and repaint.
When painting, lumps and specks of dirt have appeared on the model surface.	Paint has been insufficiently stirred or has reached the end of its life. If a tin is many months old and the paint quite thick it is often best to discard it and restock. Thorough stirring is recommended for all paints prior to application.
Matt paint dries glossy or patchy.	Insufficient stirring again. Remove with car Brake Fluid and recoat when surface has been recleaned.
Paint "skids" over surface.	Static or mould grease on model – clean with mild detergent and warm water finally wiping over with an anti-static cloth.
Second coat drags up first application.	Insufficient drying time allowed between coats. Remove with Brake Fluid and recoat. Handle fluid with care.
Removal of masking tape pulls up paint beneath.	Tape too sticky, reduce by rubbing adhesive backing prior to application or pulled away too harshly. Should be removed when paint has dried by doubling back over itself and removing gently and slowly.
First coat is thick, brush drags and uneven surface is obtained.	Paint needs thinning and re-stirring and note that too much thinners will result in general lightening of the colour. Remove with Brake Fluid and recoat.
Paint accidentally smudged over clear canopy.	Before it dries remove with a cocktail stick damped with thinners. The latter can cloud the clear part but this is restored by polishing with Duraglit.
Paint collects round edges and builds up into a ridge.	When dry, smooth with wet and dry paper recoating with thinned down colour.
Glue dropped on paint surface, accidentally.	Allow to harden, remove with knife, sand smooth and recoat.
Paint brushed over areas to be cemented.	This must be scraped off as cement will not work on a painted portion of plastic.
After 48 hours paint has still not dried out and is tacky to touch.	Either insufficiently stirred or second coat has been applied before first had really dried. The second coat prevents air from reaching the first so slowing down drying time considerably. Leave well alone for several days, handling as little as possible. Did you wash the plastic parts free of moulding oil film before starting to paint? Cleanliness comes first!

APPENDIX 3

WW1 AERO COLOUR TABLE

COLOUR NAME		METHUEN REF	HUMBROL MIX	APPLICATION
AUSTRO-HUNGARY WW1				
Prussian Blue	(1)	21F6	15/G 13 Midnight Blue	
Dark Maroon	(2)	9F6	3 parts HN5 Hull Red + 1 part HB 10 Black	Six colour hexagonal camouflage for uppersurfaces (see diagram A, page 127).
Dark Sage	(3) Dark	29F3	HG2 Dunkelgrün 72	
Mauve	(4)	15E4	2 parts N9 Mauve + 2 parts HB 10 Black	
Ultramarine	(5)	21C5		
Brown Ochre	(6)	6E5	HB2 Dark Earth	
Light Blue	(1)	25B5	Equal parts 3/G5 Brunswick Green + HB6 Sea Grey Medium + dash 14/G6 French Blue	
Pale Violet	(2) Light	14B4	46 Clover + 22/G3 Gloss White	
Light Green	(3)	28C3	2 parts MC28 Green Leather + 1 part 69/G2 Yellow	Six colour hexagonal camouflage for uppersurfaces (see diagram A, page 127).
Ochre	(4)	4B3	62/M23 Leather + dash 7 Light Buff	
Pink Grey	(5)	9B2	HB6 Sea Grey Medium + dash 19/G11 Crimson	
Blue Grey	(6)	26B3	3/G5 Brunswick Green + HB5 Sky	
Clear doped Linen		4A3	HN4 Deck Bleached Teak	
Dark Green		30(E-F)6	HB1 Dark Green + dash 69/G2 Yellow	Undersurfaces
Dark Earth		5(D-E)4	HB2 Dark Earth + dash 22/G3 Gloss White	Mottle on upper surfaces.

All finishes are semi-gloss

GREAT BRITAIN WW1				
Clear doped Linen	4A3	HN4 Deck Bleached Teak	Overall/undersurfaces
PC10	4F(2-8)	HB 15 RFC Green + dash 9/G 18 Tan	Uppersurface camouflage
PC12	8(E-F)8	HS2 16 Rust	Uppersurface camouflage
Nivo	27F3	HB1 Dark Green + dash HB7 Extra Dark Sea Grey	Overall on Night Bombers, 1918 onwards.

COLOUR NAME	METHUEN REF	HUMBROL MIX	APPLICATION
Light Grey	(B–C)1	HB6 Sea Grey Medium	Plywood panels/cowlings
Vermilion (Roundel Red)	9C8	HT6 Marker Red + dash of 69/G2 Yellow	National Insignia
Ultramarine (Roundel Blue)	20E8	M25 Matt Blue	National Insignia
Dull Red (Night Red)	8E8	HS2 16 Rust	National Insignia
Dull Blue (Night Blue)	20G4	HM12 Dark Blue	
*All finishes are semi-gloss			
FRANCE WW1			
Clear doped Linen	4A3	HN4 Deck Bleached Teak	Early overall/undersurfaces finish
Aluminium	–	3 parts HB 14 Airframe silver + 2 parts HG5 Hellblau	Overall/Undersurfaces
Dark Green	30E3	HG6 RLM Grau + dash HB8 Dark Slate Grey	Disruptive uppersurfaces camouflage on early machines. Used with Aluminium undersurfaces
Dark Earth	6E3	70 Brick Red + dash HB6 Medium Sea Grey	
Light Yellow	4B4	HB 16 Clear doped linen + dash HB6 Medium Sea Grey	Metal panels on clear doped a/c
Pale Green	30B3	HB5 Sky	Metal panels on aluminium doped a/c
Silver Grey (A)	–	HB14 Airframe + HB6 Medium Sea Grey	Mid overall/undersurfaces finish
Light Yellow (A)	4C3	HN4 Deck Bleached Teak + dash HB6 Medium Sea Grey	Mid overall/undersurfaces finish
Dark Green (A)	3F3	HG6 RLM Grau + dash HG2 Dunkelgrün	Disruptive camouflage on uppersurfaces of late a/c inc. those in Belgium, Italian and AEF Services.
†Light Green (A)	3E4	HB8 Dark Slate Grey + dash HB5 Sky	
†Beige (A)	5D5	63 Sand + dash 62/M23 Leather	Used with Silver Grey or Light Yellow undersurfaces
†Dark Brown (A)	5E3	10/G9 Service Brown + dash HF6 Chocolate	
Black	–	21/G4 Black	
Roundel Red	10D8	19/G1 Bright Red	National Insignia
Roundel Blue	23D4	48 Mediterranean Blue + dash 40/G 14 Pale Grey	

†N.B. (A) These finishes contain Aluminium (HB 14) in sufficient quantity to just begin to show an Aluminium sheen in with the colour.
*All finishes are semi-matt

APPENDIX 3 Continued

COLOUR NAME		METHUEN REF	HUMBROL MIX	APPLICATION
GERMANY WW1				
Dark Violet		17F8	68 Purple	
Dark Green		25D8	3/G5 Brunswick Green + dash 14/G6 French Blue	Disruptive camouflage on uppersurfaces eg. Albatros DIII/DV
Pale Blue		23B3	47/G10 Sea Blue + dash HB6 Medium Sea Grey	Undersurfaces
Dark Brown		6E8	HB2 Dark Earth + dash 18/G17 Orange	
Dark Green		26F3	HG1 Schwarzgrün	Disruptive camouflage on uppersurfaces, eg. Fokker DIII, Halberstadt DIII etc.
Mauve		18D6	68 Purple + dash 14/G6 French Blue	
Pale Blue		24B4	HG5 Hellblau 65	Undersurfaces
Grey		1(C-D)1	HB6 Medium Sea Grey	Metal panels, cowlings
Bright Green		26D8/E8	2 Emerald + dash 48 Mediterranean Blue	Tail colours: Jasta 5
Rose Red	(1)	11B8	19/G1 Bright Red	
Grey Blue	(2)	21E7	67/M22 Tank Grey	Handpainted Hexagonal finish used with black (3) on upper and lower surfaces and used on AEG, Gotha Bombers etc. (see diagram **B**)
Greyish Magenta	(4)	14E5	46 Clover	
Dark Green		26F5	3/G9 Brunswick Green	
Blue	(1)	21D4	67/M22 Tank Grey	
Turquoise	(2)	(24-25)E7	3/G5 Brunswick Green + dash 14/G6 French Blue	4 colour printed fabric uppersurfaces (see diagram **C**). Fighters and two-seaters
Beige	(3)	(4-5)D4	62/M23 Leather + dash 7 Light Buff	
Green	(4)	(29-30)D5	HD1 Grey Green	
Pale Blue	(1)	23D4	HB 13 Azure Blue	
Green	(2)	26D4	3/G5 Brunswick Green + dash HB5 Sky	4 colour printed fabric lower surfaces (see diagram **C**). Fighters and two-seaters
Ochre	(3)	(4-5)C7	63/M14 Sand	
Rose	(4)	11B5	61/M7 Flesh	
Violet	(2)	17E(5-6)	68 Purple	
Khaki	(3)	(4-5)D6	62/M23 Leather	
Green	(4)	28D(5-6)	HF2 Vert	5 colour printed fabric uppersurfaces (see diagram **D**). Fighters and two-seaters
Turquoise	(1)	24(E-F)6	3/G3 Brunswick Green + dash 14/G6 French Blue	

COLOUR NAME

COLOUR NAME		METHUEN REF	HUMBROL MIX
Blue	(5)	21E(6–7)	67/M22 Tank Grey
Magenta	(2)	(14-15)D4	46 Clover
Wheat	(3)	(4-5)B6	62/M23 Leather + dash 7 Light Buff
Ruby	(4)	12(C-D)5	HG9 German Purple
Green	(1)	(24-35)D4	3/G3 Brunswick Green + dash 14/G6 French Blue
Blue	(5)	(21-22)D6	67/M22 Tank Grey

All finishes are semi-gloss

APPLICATION

5 colour printed fabric lower surfaces (see diagram **D**). Fighters and two-seaters

PATTERN REPEATS

C   D

PATTERN REPEATS

A   B

NB
HEXAGONS
15" ACROSS FLATS

ITALY WW1

	METHUEN REF	HUMBROL MIX
Dark Green	30F7	HG8 German Green + dash 24/M15 Yellow
Light Green	30D6	38 Lime + dash HB6 Sea Grey Medium
Sand	4A5	HB 16 Clear doped Linen
National Red	11D8	HG9 German Purple
National Green	28E7	38 Lime + dash 64/M13 Light Grey
Silver Grey	24C3	HG3 Hellgrau 76
Silver Grey	–	HB 14 Airframe Silver + HB6 Sea Grey medium

All finishes are semi-gloss

Mottle finish on fighters (uppersurfaces)

Roundel colours and/or bands on lower wing surfaces
Uppersurfaces
Undersurfaces/overall, eg, Nieuport 17 etc.

APPENDIX 4

WW2 AERO COLOUR TABLE

COLOUR NAME	METHUEN REF	HUMBROL MIX	APPLICATION
AUSTRALIA WW2			
Foliage Green	3F4	66/M21 Olive drab	Used overall or as disruptive pattern with Dark Earth
Dark Earth	5(E-F)4	HB2	Used as disruptive pattern with Foliage or Dark Green
Dark Green	30(F-G)2	HB1	Used with Dark Earth as disruptive camouflage pattern
Pale Blue	23A2	47/G10 Sea Blue + dash 34/M10 Matt White	
(Later Azure Blue)	21B5	HB13	Undersurfaces
Roundel Blue	20F5	HM12 Dark Blue	National Insignia
All finishes matt			
GREAT BRITAIN WW2			
Dark Earth	5(E-F)4	HB2	Used with Dark Green as disruptive pattern: European
Light Earth	5D4	4 parts HB2 Dark Earth + 1 part 34/M10 Matt White	Used with Light Green as disruptive pattern on lower wings of biplanes
Dark Green	30(F-G)2	HB1	Used with Dark Earth as disruptive pattern: European
Light Green	30F4	4 parts HB2 Dark Green + 1 part 34/M10 Matt White	Used with Light Earth as disruptive pattern on lower wings of biplanes
Sky	29B2	HB5	Used on undersurfaces – European/ Coastal Command FAA etc.
Ocean Grey	23E3	HB3	Used with Dark Green as disruptive pattern with HB6 undersurfaces
Sea Grey Medium	22D3	HB6	Undersurfaces
Dark Sea Grey	21E3	HN2 Dark Grey	Used on uppersurfaces, Coastal Command/FAA
Light Slate Grey	26E3	4 parts HG6RLM Grau + 1 part 24/M15 Matt Yellow	Used on lowersurfaces, Coastal Command/FAA.

COLOUR NAME	METHUEN REF	HUMBROL MIX	APPLICATION
Extra Dark Sea Grey	21F3	HB7	
Dark Slate Grey	29F2	HB8	
Mid Stone	4D7	HB12	Used with Dark Earth as disruptive camouflage – Overseas
Azure Blue	21B5	HB13	Undersurfaces: Overseas
PRU Blue	23E4	HX3	Photo Reconnaissance – overall
Roundel Red	10C6	Matt Red 60/M12	National Insignia 1930–1936
Roundel Blue		20E8	Matt Blue 25/M11
Roundel Red	8D7	HS216 Rust	National Insignia
Roundel Blue	HM12 Dark Blue	1941-1946	
Roundel/Trainer Yellow	(4-5)A8	Matt Trainer Yellow 24/M15	Trainers – undersides
Aluminium	20F5	4 parts HB14 Silver + 1 part 64/M13 Light Grey	
Night	–	HB10 Night Black	Overall and undersurfaces
Aircraft Grey Green	27D3	HD1	Cockpit Interiors – most a/c
Sky Grey	22C2	HX5 Light Aircraft Grey + dash 23/M8	Used on undersurfaces FAA, 1939-1940
All finishes are matt		Duck Egg Blue	
GERMANY WW2			
00 Wasserhell	None	35/GV1 Clear Gloss	A clear varnish additive to achieve a gloss finish.
02 Silber	None	11/G8 Silver Fox (gloss)	A top coat and/or primer colour. Used also as a marine anti-fouling finish for floats and hulls
02 RLM Grau	1(D-E)3 to 27(D-E)2	HG6	Marine camouflage colour; also used as an internal finish and as a general colour on some land-planes, also cockpit areas
03 Silber	None	HB14 Silver (semi-gloss) + dash of HB6 Sea Grey Medium	Early overall finish for all types of surface later replaced by colour 63
04 Gelb	4(A-B)8	10 parts 24/M15 Trainer Yellow + 1 part HM10 Scarlet	For identification and fuel grade markings, also used for marine trainers, and "theatre" markings.
05 Rahm	3B5	5 parts MC25 Unbleached Linen + 1 part 24/M15 Trainer Yellow	Early overall finish for gliders and sailplanes
21 Weiss	None	Matt 34/M10 White	Identification colour/markings, for internal instruments and aircraft systems (ie, fuel, air and hydraulic pipes). Also external for warnings etc. National insignia colours.
22 Schwarz	None	Matt 33/M6 Black	Early night camouflage
23 Rot	(9-10)B8	HM9 Scarlet + dash of 34/M10 White	National insignia colour

APPENDIX 4 *Continued*

GERMANY cont. WW2

COLOUR NAME	METHUEN REF	HUMBROL MIX	APPLICATION
24 Dunkelblau	21(F-G) (5-6)	1 part MC8 French Blue + 1 part MC12 Prussian Dragoon Blue	Limited overall aircraft for pre-war machines, sometimes with 23 Rot until banned in 1937
25 Hellgrun	(25-26)D(7-8)	1 part MC12 Prussian Dragoon blue + 1 part MC7 Dragoon Green	
26 Braun	(7-8)(E-F)8	HM21 Leather	
27 Gelb	5(B-C)7	5 parts 24/M15 Trainer Yellow + 1 part 33/M6 Black	Sometimes used for "theatre" markings
28 Weinrot	11D(7-8)	5 parts MC6 Brown + 2 parts HM9 Scarlet	Used for marking walkway areas and trim tabs
41 Mittelgrau	24D2	64/M13 Light Grey + dash of HB10 Night Black	Internal finish also a primer colour. A lighter grey 1(B-C) 1 used for instrument panels up to 1942
61 Dunkelbraun	6(F-G)4-5)	5 parts HM21 Leather + 1 part 33/M6 Black	Camouflage colour used mostly on bombers with 62 and 63.
62 Grun	7(E-F)3	HD5 Interior Green	Camouflage colour used mostly on bombers with 61 and 63
63 Hellgrau	(1-2)(B-C)2	HN4 Deck Bleached Teak + dash of HB5 Sky and HG3 Hellgrau	Overall aircraft colour in place of 03 and camouflage colour used mostly on bombers with 61 and 62.
65 Hellblau	24B(2-3)	5 parts HG3 Hellgrau + 2 parts MC12 Prussian Dragoon Blue	Undersurface camouflage colour used throughout WW2
66 Schwarzgrau	21F(1-2)	67/M22 Tank Grey + dash HB6 Sea Grey Medium	Camouflage colour. Interior of cockpits for high altitude aircraft, armour plate colour
70 Schwarzgrun	28B2	HG15 RFC Green + dash of HB1 Dark Green and HU2 Olive Drab 41	Basic landplane camouflage colour usually used with 70. Also used for prop blades when mixed with 00
71 Dunkelgrün	(29-30)F3	HG2 Dunkelgrün 71 + dash HB8 Dark Slate Grey	Basic landplane camouflage colour usually used with 70
72 Grun	25G3	5 parts 67/M22 Tank Grey + 2 parts MC7 Dragoon Green	Basic camouflage colour on seaplanes or landplanes operating over water. Usually used with 73
73 Grun	25(E-F)3	4 parts HG2 Dunkelgrün 71 + 1 part 67/M22 Tank Grey	Basic camouflage colour on seaplanes or landplanes operating over water. Usually used with 72

GERMANY cont. WW2

COLOUR NAME	METHUEN REF	HUMBROL MIX	APPLICATION
74 Dunkelgrau	21(E-F)3	HG4	Camouflage colour often used with 75 and 76. Only for fighters, night fighters and Zerstorer aircraft.
75 Mittelgrau	23D(2-3)	3 parts HG4 + 1 part 34/M10 White	Camouflage colour often used with 74 and 76. Same applications as 74.
76 Hellgrau	(23-23)A2	HB4 Duck Egg Blue + dash of 22/G3 Gloss White	Undersurface colour. Used on fighters, night fighters and Zerstorer aircraft.
77 Hellgrau	30C(1-2)	8 parts 22/G3 White + 1 part 21/G4 Black	Only for lettering and national insignia in night operations, on colour 22.
78 Himmelblau	23B4	2 parts 48 Mediterranean Blue + 1 part 22/G3 White + dash HB6 Sea Grey Medium	Undersurface colour for use with desert colours 79 and 80.
79 Sandbraun	(4-5)D6	63/M14 Sand	Uppersurface colour. Used with 78 and 80
80 Olivegrun	4(F-G)8	HB 15 RFC Green + dash HB2 Dark Earth	Uppersurface colour. Used only over 79
81 Dunkelgrun	(27-28)F6	3/G5 Brunswick Green + dash HB1 Dark Green	Late war upper surface camouflage colour. Used singly or with 82. Undersurface colour 65.
82 Dunkelgrun	(27-28)E8	MC28 Green Leather	Later was uppersurface camouflage colour. Used only with colour 81. Undersurface colour 65.
99 Gelb/Grun	1B6	Suggest using a tint of HD4 Zinc Chromate	Primer enamel and anodic finish. Often used on cowling fasteners and other internal components having no special colour importance

*All finishes semi-gloss

FRANCE WW2

COLOUR NAME	METHUEN REF	HUMBROL MIX	APPLICATION
Kaki	4F2	HF1	Uppersurface disruptive pattern, used with Vert, Terre Foncee, Gris Bleu Fonce
Vert	27D6	HF2	Used with above. Overall colour on certain a/c and cockpit interiors.
Terre Foncee	6(E-F)7	HF3	Uppersurface disruptive pattern, see above
Gris Bleu Clair	23D3	HF4	Undersurfaces
Gris Bleu Fonce	21E3	HF5	Uppersurface disruptive pattern. See above. Also used as basic finish on Vichy a/c.
Chocolate (gloss)	6F4 (Approx.)	HF6	Pre 1939 Bombers – overall or sometimes with Black undersurfaces.
Vert (gloss)	27(E-F)8	HF2 + dash 2 Emerald + dash 21/G Black	Pre 1939 Fighters – overall.

APPENDIX 4 continued

COLOUR NAME	METHUEN REF	HUMBROL MIX	APPLICATION
FRANCE WW2 continued			
Night Blue	None	HD3	Cockpit interiors
Roundel Blue	23D4	48 Mediterranean Blue + dash 40/G14 Pale Grey	National Insignia
Roundel Red	10D8	19/G1 Bright Red	Used up to 1942 with red as stripes on nose and tail.
Vichy Yellow	3A8	24/M15 Trainer Yellow	
ITALY WW2			
Mottle Green	1E4	H11	Overseas – Used over Sand
Upper Green	28D5 (Approx.)	H12	Home based – Used over Mottle Green See above.
Overall Green	26E4 (Approx.)	H13	Overall upper surfaces.
Bright green	27D4/5	HD2	Cockpit interiors
Sand	(3-4)B4	H14	Uppersurface used with Mottle Green above or over Mottle Green
Grey	None 2C(2-3)	H15	Undersurfaces

For National identity colours, refer to WW1 columns

COLOUR NAME	METHUEN REF	HUMBROL MIX	APPLICATION
RUSSIA WW2			
Topside Green	28E4	HT1	Uppersurfaces
Undersides Blue	24B4 (Approx.)	HT2	Undersurfaces
Surface Grey	None	HT3	Uppersurfaces – Winter
Subframe Grey	9B8	HT4	Interiors of cockpit, wheel wells etc.
Marker Red	2A8	HT5	National Insignia and markings
Insignia Yellow		HT6	
JAPAN WW2			
Green N1	24F3	HJ1	Uppersurfaces – Navy a/c
Green A3	30E4 (Approx.)	HJ3	Uppersurfaces Army a/c, and as disruptive pattern over natural metal airframe
Grey A/N2	1(A-B)1	HJ2	Undersurfaces Navy and Army a/c
Mauve N9	None 16D3	HJ4	Overall – Float planes
Brown N17	5D4 (Approx.)	HJ5	Army a/c used with Green N1 as disruptive pattern – uppersurfaces
Roundel Red (Hinomaru)	8D7	HS2 16 Rust	National Insignia
Interior Green/Blue	None	HB13 Azure Blue + 1 part 35/GV1 gloss	Interior cockpits, wheel wells

COLOUR NAME	METHUEN REF	HUMBROL MIX	APPLICATION
UNITED STATES OF AMERICA WW2			
Olive Drab 41 ANA 613	30F6	HU2	Uppersurfaces – 1943 onwards
Medium Green 42 ANA 612	28F6	HU1	Uppersurfaces fighters in Europe from 1943 (used as patches over OD41 on bombers) Interior cockpit 1941 onwards
Interior Green ANA 611	30F8	HD5	
Middlestone ANA 615	4(D-E)4	HB12 Mid Stone	
Sand 49 ANA	6C3 (Approx.)	1 part HB2 Dark Earth + 3 parts 34/M10 Matt White	
Dark Earth ANA 617	5(E-F)4	HB2	
Neutral Gray 43	24E2 (Approx.)	HU3	Undersurfaces: On some a/c replaced by Light Gray after 1943 1939-41. Overall. Then undersurfaces until 1943
Light Gray	22C2 (Approx.)	HU6	
Blue Gray	22F3 (Approx.)	HU3 Neutral Gray + dash of 34/M10 Matt White	
Dark Gull Gray	2(D-E)3 (Approx.)	HT4 Subframe Gray	
Light Gull Gray ANA 620	2(B-C)2 (Approx.)	3 parts HU6 Light Gray + 1 part 34/M10 Matt White	
Aircraft Gray	24C2 (Approx.)	MC4 British Gray (gloss)	
Engine Gray (gloss)	20F2	Equal parts 5 Dark Gray + 21/G4 Black	Engine crankcases
Non Specular Sea Blue	22F4	HU4	Uppersurface US Navy – January 1943 onwards
Intermediate Blue	22D4 (Approx.)	HU5	USN 1943/44 Fins/Rudders, side of fuselage used with Non Spec Sea Blue and White Undersurfaces
Azure Blue	21B5	HB13 + 1 part 34/M10 Matt White	
Semi Gloss Sea Blue	22G4 (Approx.)	HB1 + part 49/MV1 Matt Varnish	
Glossy Sea Blue	22G4 (Approx.)	HB9	
Sky Blue	28B3	HB5 Sky	
Insignia Blue 47 ANA 605	21HB (Approx.)	HM12 Dark Blue	Undersurfaces
Insignia Red 45 ANA 618	10D8	19/G1 Bright Red	National Insignia
Bright Red	9A8	60/M12 Matt Red	National Insignia
Ident' Yellow 48	4A8	H5 220 Signal Yellow	
International Orange	7B8	18/G17 Orange	
Zinc Chromate	None / 2C6 Approx.	HD4	Pre-1941 interior of cockpit, wheel wells, etc.

APPENDIX 5

CONTEMPORARY AERO COLOUR TABLE

COLOUR NAME	METHUEN REF	HUMBROL MIX	APPLICATION
NATO (RAF AND MOST EUROPEAN AIR FORCES) CONTEMPORARY			
Dark Green	30(F-G)2	HX1	Uppersurface disruptive camouflage finish.
Dark Sea Grey	21E3	HX2	Gloss or matt finish
PRU Blue	23E4	HX3	Overall until 1948 then undersurfaces
Sea Grey	22D3	HX4	Undersurfaces
Light Aircraft Grey	None	HX5	Undersurfaces 1960 onwards with Dark Green and Dark Sea Grey
Extra Dark Sea Grey	(24(C-D)2)	HX6	Overall Navy a/c. Also with white undersurfaces
Sky	29B2	HB5	Undersurfaces AEW types
SWEDEN CONTEMPORARY			
322M Light Green	30F5	HB8 Dark Slate Grey	Disruptive four colour
326M Dark Olive Green	26E3	HF1 Schwarzgrün	camouflage on uppersurfaces.
093M Black	–	HB10 Night Black	Viggen, Bulldog etc.
507M Brown	5F5	HB2 Dark Earth + touch of Red	
058M Blue/Grey	23F2	HB3 Ocean Grey	Undersurfaces
Dayglo Orange	None	Fluorescent Blaze	Panels and numerals
UNITED STATES CONTEMPORARY			
34079 Dark Green	30F4/5	HU7	Basic Tactical Scheme
34102 Green OD	30E6 (Approx.)	HU8	Disruptive pattern on uppersurfaces.
30219 Tan	5E(A-5)	HU9	With 36622 Gray or Black undersurfaces
36622 Gray	1B1	HU10	Undersurfaces
34159 Blue Green	27E3	2 parts HD1 Aircraft Gray Green + 1 part HB1 Dark Green	Bomber scheme. Disruptive pattern on uppersurfaces with 34079 Dark Green.
24201 Tan	4E4	HM7 Khaki Drab	Black, Gray or White Undersurfaces
37038 Black	None	HU12 Night Black	Undersurfaces
30140 Brown	6E5	2 parts HU9 Tan 80219 + 1 part HB2 Dark Earth	Asia Minor Schemes. Disruptive pattern on uppersurfaces with 34079 Dark Green.
20400 Tan	5C5	HG7 German Pale Yellow	Gray undersurfaces

Colour	Code	Reference	Notes
Insignia Red	10D8	19/G1 Bright Red	National Insignia
Insignia Blue	21H8 (Approx.)	HM12 Dark Blue	Interior of wheel wells, also overall undersides
Insignia White	1A1	HU11 Airframe White	Uppersurfaces US Navy/Marines used with White undersurfaces
Gulf Gray	22(B-C)2	3 parts HU6 Light Gray + 1 part 34/M10 Matt White	Overall on some a/c, eg, F15 Eagle
Air Superiority Blue	22A(3-4)(Approx.)	47/G10 Sea Blue	

ISRAEL CONTEMPORARY

Colour	Code	Reference	Notes
Green 34227	28E6	Vert HF2	Disruptive camouflage on uppersurfaces
Earth 30219	6(D-E)4	HB2 Dark Earth + dash of 34/M10 Matt White	Lower surfaces
Middlestone 33531	4B2	63 Sand + 34/M10 Matt White	
Pale Blue 35662	24A3	65 Aircraft Blue + 34/M10 Matt White	

APPENDIX 6

HOBBYPOXY COLOUR MIXES

Hobbypoxy Products, the American makers of what are probably the best-known and most widely used epoxy enamels, have published over a number of years a series of mixes to produce standard aircraft colours. The formulae were developed using standard Hobbypoxy colours and the same mix used with other paint brands will NOT result in the same final colours. Matt colours should include Part B Flat Hardener. FS = Federal Standard reference.

U.S. Insignia Colours

Insignia Red (FS 11136 gloss, FS 31136 matt) up to 1942
15 parts	H66 Dark Red
1 part	H65 Bright Red

(May '42 to end of WW2 see R.A.F. Red)

Insignia White (FS 17875 gloss, FS 37875 matt) WW2
½ pt. (8 fl.oz)	H10 White
16 drops	H81 Black
6 drops	H49 Cub Yellow
4 drops	H33 Stinson Green

Insignia Blue (FS 15044 gloss, FS 35044 matt) WW2
3 parts	H24 Dark Blue
2 parts	H67 Maroon
1 part	H81 Black

Insignia Blue (Sea Blue) (FS 15042 gloss)
3 parts	H81 Black
2 parts	H33 Stinson Green
1 part	H24 Dark Blue

U.S. Navy Fighters, 1930-43)

Gloss Light Gray (ANA 512)
9 parts	H70 Gray
5 parts	H10 White
1 part	H55 Cream

Matt Light Gray (ANA 602)
50 parts	H10 White
21 parts	H70 Gray
2 parts	H66 Dark Red
1 part	H49 Cub Yellow

Matt Blue-Gray (ANA 603)
10 parts	H70 Gray
3 parts	H81 Black

Olive Drab 41, WW2 (pre-1964 FS 34087)
2 parts	H66 Dark Red
2 parts	H81 Black
1 part	H10 White
1 part	H49 Cub Yellow

Neutral Gray 43, WW2 (FS 36173)
4 parts	H10 White
2 parts	H81 Black
1 part	H26 Light Blue

Sea Blue WW2 (FS 35042)
3 parts	H81 Black
2 parts	H33 Stinson Green
1 part	H24 Dark Blue

Intermediate Blue WW2
4 parts	H70 Gray
3 parts	H66 Dark Red
1 part	H24 Dark Blue

Matt White WW2
½ pint (8 fl.oz.)	H10 White
16 drops	H81 Black
6 drops	H49 Cub Yellow
4 drops	H33 Stinson Green

Light Gull Gray WW2
50 parts	H10 White
21 parts	H70 Gray
2 parts	H66 Dark Red
1 part	H49 Cub Yellow

Interior Green 611, WW2 (cockpit interior metalwork)
5 parts	H49 Cub Yellow
3 parts	H47 Bright Yellow
2 parts	H33 Stinson Green
1 part	H81 Black

Zinc Chromate Primer (Yellow) WW2 (general interior metalwork)
3 parts	H47 Bright Yellow
3 parts	H49 Cub Yellow
2 parts	H70 Gray

"European One" (current)

Light Green (FS 34102)
4 parts	H65 Bright Red
3 parts	H49 Cub Yellow
3 parts	H81 Black
2 parts	H33 Stinson Green
1 part	H70 Gray
1 part	H10 White

Dark Green (FS 34092)
4 parts	H33 Stinson Green
4 parts	H81 Black
3 parts	H47 Bright Yellow
2 parts	H70 Gray

Dark Gray (FS 36081)
6 parts	H81 Black
5 parts	H70 Gray
1 part	H47 Bright Yellow
1 part	H66 Dark Red

R.A.F. Insignia Colours

R.A.F. Red
20 parts	H65 Bright Red
3 parts	H66 Dark Red

2 parts	H57 Orange
1 part	H81 Black
1 part	H10 White

R.A.F. Blue

11 parts	H24 Dark Blue
2 parts	H81 Black
1 part	H65 Bright Red

R.A.F. Yellow

9 parts	H49 Cub Yellow
7 parts	H47 Bright Yellow
3 parts	H55 Cream
2 parts	H66 Dark Red

Dark Earth (early WW2)

4 parts	H65 Bright Red
2 parts	H49 Cub Yellow
1 part	H81 Black
1 part	H70 Gray

Dark Green (early WW2)

6 parts	H66 Dark Red
2 parts	H33 Stinson Green
1 part	H49 Cub Yellow
1 part	H81 Black
1 part	H10 White

Sky Type S (early WW2)

5 parts	H10 White
1 part	H26 Light Blue
1 part	H70 Gray

Medium Sea Grey (1942 on)

3 parts	H70 Gray
1 part	H10 White

Ocean Grey (1942 on)

7 parts	H70 Gray
2 parts	H81 Black
1 part	H33 Stinson Green

Middle Stone (1942 on)

3 parts	H49 Cub Yellow
4 parts	H70 Gray
1 part	H65 Bright Red
1 part	H10 White

Luftwaffe WW2 Marking Colours
Yellow 04

40 parts	H49 Cub Yellow
2 parts	H70 Gray
1 part	H65 Bright Red

Red 23

32 parts	H65 Bright Red
8 parts	H66 Dark Red
1 part	H47 Bright Yellow
1 part	H10 White

Dark Blue 24

3 parts	H24 Dark Blue
5 parts	H65 Bright Red
1 part	H10 White

Black-Green 70 (1937-40)

5 parts	H81 Black
2 parts	H33 Stinson Green

Dark Green 71 (1937-40)

7 parts	H65 Bright Red
4 parts	H33 Stinson Green
3 parts	H81 Black
3 parts	H47 Bright Yellow

Light Blue 65 (1937-40)

10 parts	H70 Gray
7 parts	H10 White
2 parts	H26 Light Blue
1 part	H33 Stinson Green

Elm Grey 02 (1937-40)

20 parts	H70 Gray
2 parts	H49 Cub Yellow
2 parts	H65 Bright Red
1 part	H33 Stinson Green

Grey Green 74 (1940-44)

6 parts	H81 Black
2 parts	H70 Gray
1 part	H33 Stinson Green
1 part	H47 Bright Yellow

Grey Violet 75 (1940-45)

2 parts	H81 Black
1 part	H70 Gray
1 part	H65 Bright Red
1 part	H10 White

Light Blue 76 (1940-45)

½ pint (8 fl.oz.)	H10 White
3 teaspoons	H70 Gray
2 teaspoons	H26 Light Blue
2 teaspoons	H81 Black
2 teaspoons	H33 Stinson Green

Dark Green 82 (1940-45)

4 parts	H81 Black
4 parts	H33 Stinson Green
3 parts	H65 Bright Red
2 parts	H49 Cub Yellow

Japanese
Light Grey N10 (1933-41)

16 parts	H10 White
13 parts	H70 Gray
8 parts	H55 Cream
1 part	H47 Bright Yellow

Black Green N1 (1942-46)

6 parts	H33 Stinson Green
2 parts	H81 Black
1 part	H65 Bright Red

Grey Green N4 (1942-46) cockpit interiors

20 parts	H70 Gray
2 parts	H49 Cub Yellow
2 parts	H65 Bright Red
1 part	H33 Stinson Green

Primer   (Translucent   Blue)   (1942-46)   interior
metalwork

5 parts	H24 Dark Blue
2 parts	H99 Custom Metaliser
1 part	H33 Stinson Green

Dark Green A1 (1942-46)

6 parts	H81 Black
4 parts	H33 Stinson Green
2 parts	H66 Dark Red
1 part	H49 Cub Yellow

Light Grey A9 (1942-46)

28 parts	H10 White
10 parts	H70 Gray
6 parts	H55 Cream
1 part	H47 Bright yellow

APPENDIX 7

SCALE COLOUR REFERENCES

"Colours for Specific Purposes"
British Standard 371C: 1964 (UDC 5366) is available from *British Standards House, 2 Park Street, London W1*. The booklet contains 100 gloss colour chips of British colour standards and also includes useful notes, tables and appendices.
"Federal Standards No. 595a"
A catalogue of 437 colour chips 1in. × ½in. applicable to USAA/USN aircraft and equipment. It is avail able from *Specifications Activity, Printed Materials Supply Division, Building 197, Naval Weapons Plant, Washington DC 20407, USA*. You should write first to confirm postage rates and current price. Otherwise from *American Information Retrieval Service, 22 Roland Gardens, London SW7 3PL*.
"United States Camouflage WWII"
An American publication containing 20 colour chips. It is available from *Scale Reproductions, 1313 West Abram, Arlington, Texas 76010, USA*.

"British Aviation Colours of WW2"
Volume 3 in the RAF Museum Series, published by *Arms and Armour Press, 2-6 Hampstead High Street, London NW3 1PR*.
Contains 32 colour chips applicable to WW2 RAF aircraft. It retails at £4.45.
"The Modeller's Luftwaffe Painting Guide"
By J. R. Smith, C. G. Pentland and R. P. Lutz. Contains accurate colour chips for 30 WW2 shades. Published by *Kookaburra Technical Publications Pty Ltd., Melbourne, Australia*.
"Methuen Handbook of Colour"
By A. Kornerup and Wanscher. Contains chips showing all variations of colour tone along with detailed annotations. Published by *Methuen & Co. Ltd., 11 New Fetter Lane, London EC4*.

APPENDIX 8

ARMOURED FIGHTING VEHICLE COLOUR TABLE

COLOUR NAME	METHUEN REF	HUMBROL MIX	APPLICATION
BRITISH ARMY 1940-1977			
Deep Bronze Green	30G8 (Approx.)	HP4	Overall Post War
Dark Green	30F4	HB1	Overall WW2 and post war
Light Olive Green	30E6	HB1 Dark Green + dash of 34/M10 Matt White	Used with Dark Green as disruptive pattern, Universal Carriers etc.
Desert Yellow	4C6 (Approx.)	HM1	Middle East Finishes – WW2
Dark Earth	None	HB2	
Charcoal Grey	24E3 (Approx.)	4 parts M4 Panzer Grey + 1 part 24/M15 Trainer Yellow	
Smoke Grey	23C6		Currently used as camouflage over Matt Green
Black	None	33/M6 Black	
GERMAN ARMY WW2			
Sand Tan Primer	None	HP1 Overall Sand	Factory colour
Desert Yellow	None	HM2 Afrika Korps Desert Yellow	Overall desert finish or as base for Mottle
Panzer Blue Grey	23E3	HM4 Panzer Grey	General Overall finish
Dark Green	30F4	HB1	Camouflage colour
Green Overspray	29F6 (approx.)	HP3 Camouflage Medium Green	Camouflage over sand-tan finishes
Red Brown	7D5	HP2 Camouflage Red Brown	Camouflage colour used with sand tan and green
US ARMY 1940-1977			
US Army Olive Drab Green 34127	3F4 (Approx.)	HM3 Olive Drab	Overall finish WW2
	1E8	HI1 Mottle Green + dash G34/M10 Matt White	Camouflage used in 1974 on vehicles in W. Germany belonging to the US Army's 7th Army. Used on M113 carriers etc.
Brown 30117	6E6	2 parts HU9 Tan 80219 + 1 part HB2 Dark Earth	Winter US and Europe – Verdant colour scheme, used with black as disruptive
Brown 37038	4D3 (Approx.)	HM7 Khaki Drab	
Black 37038	None	33/M6 Black	
Forest Green 34079	30F6	2 parts HB2 Dark Green + 1 part Matt Black	camouflage. M113, M106, M125 vehicles etc.

APPENDIX 9

GERMAN LOZENGE PATTERNING

The four colours used were:

1. Ochre
2. Pale apple green
3. Blue green
4. Mauve

On undersides the last two colours were in paler shades.

Make a master pattern to the scale you require; this corresponds to the width of the fabric panels in the full-size aircraft. Pattern lines are $1\frac{1}{8}$ inch apart for 1:48 scale, $\frac{3}{4}$ inch apart for 1:72 scale, and $1\frac{11}{16}$ inch apart for 1:32 scale.

The task which puts many many modellers off First World War period model aircraft is the exotic and intricate lozenge-pattern camouflage carried by many German warplanes of the time. On the real aircraft this effect was obtained by using fabric on which the pattern was printed, in an endlessly repeated pattern, rather like curtain material. You can use the system shown here to draw out and paint in an accurate lozenge scheme without too much trouble, though careful marking out is necessary.

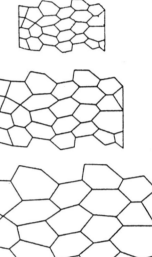

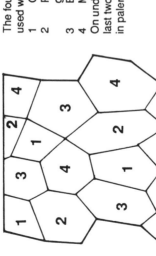

After painting the entire wing surface with one of the pale colours, trace the master pattern on to tracing paper. Draw a series of lines across the wing to depict the panel lines, place the tracing paper master in position to line up with the wing lines, then use a sharp pencil to trace the pattern through to the wings. Move the pattern up one section and repeat. Do this for each set of panel lines until the wing is covered. Then choose the easiest of the three remaining colours to identify, say the green, and fill in the lozenges which should be green, making sure the repetition is in regular sequence. Then apply the remaining colours, also in a regularly repeated sequence. It is a long repetitive job but worthwhile for the end result.

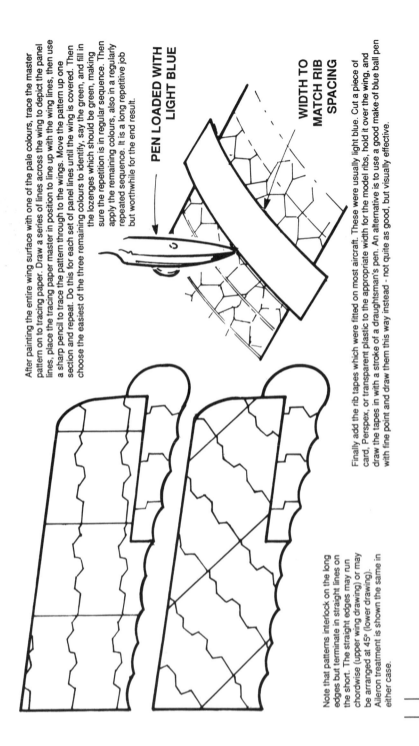

PEN LOADED WITH
LIGHT BLUE

WIDTH TO
MATCH RIB
SPACING

Finally add the rib tapes which were fitted on most aircraft. These were usually light blue. Cut a piece of card, Perspex, or transparent plastic to the appropriate width for the model ribs, hold it over the wing, and draw the tapes in with a stroke of a draughtsman's pen. An alternative is to use a good make of blue ball pen with fine point and draw them this way instead - not quite as good, but visually effective.

Note that patterns interlock on the long edges but terminate in straight lines on the short. The straight edges may run chordwise (upper wing drawing) or may be arranged at 45° (lower drawing). Aileron treatment is shown the same in either case.

INDEX

Acid primers 51
Acrylics 15
Adhesive "tack" 67
Adornment 7
Aerokote 23
Aeropoxy 47
Aerosols 36
Agitators 10
Airbrushes 31
Airbrushing and Spray Painting Manual 31–65
Airfix 52
Aluminium loaded epoxy 45
Artists inks 21
Badger Airtex 117
Balsa wood models 41
Barrier lacquer 80
Blu-tak 58
Brush storage and cleaning 28–29
Butyrate 14
Camouflage dope 12
Camouflage techniques 65
Canal barges 96
Cellulose lacquers 11
Chartpak 70
Clear varnish 9
Coloured primers 48
Colour matching 61
Colour perspective 61
Commercial transfers 76
Compasses 39
Compressors 34
Compressor/airbrush compatibility 35
Concealment 6
Contents 5
Co-ordinated colours 88
Crêpe paper tapes 67
Curing temperature 63
Custom paints 118
Cyanide risks 16–64
Daler 15–25
Dalon 26
D.B.I. PAINTS 9
Dispersion head 10
Double action airbrushes 32

Drying times 59
Dry brush method 110
Enamel 8
Environmental protection 6
Epoxides 19
Epoxy/polyester non compatibility 48
Expanded polystyrene 54
Fabric dyes 22
Fabric painting 116
Fairground models 96
Feathered edges 65
Figure painting 112
Film/paint matching 84
Finishing resins 45
Flexing additives 13
Frisk film 70
Fuel proofers 13, 17, 18, 22
Furrowing 30
Garnet paper 40
Grain fillers 42
Greenstuff 53
G.R.P. 17, 18
Grumbacher 27
Hangar rash 50
Health and safety 16, 35
Heat resistant finishes 21, 97
Hobbypoxy 63
Home made transfers 76
Hot air curing 60
Humbrol 8
Inhalation risks 16, 64
K & B SUPER POXY 46
Letrajet 36
Letraset 70
Lexan 94
Light industrial spray guns 33
Liquid masking 71
Live steam 96
Loco trim lines 99
Low temp storage 60
Mahl stick, use of 90
Masking off 65
Masking tapes 67
Maskol 71
Meccanorma 70

M.E.K. 30
Metal finishing 51
Metalflake 119
Microballoons 50
MICRO SYSTEM 111
Mini spray guns 33
Mixed material finishing 53
Model railways 109
Motor trade supplies 12
Multi stripe lines 101
Narrow masking tapes 68–70
Needleless airbrushes 33
Non-bloom thinners 13
Obechi covering 43
One seventy second scale models 103
Opalescent colours 120
Optical illusions 79
Orange peel 59
Overcoating 60
Overspray 97
Oxidisation 51
Paint brushes:
    cleaning 20
    Goat hair 26
    Hog's hair 29
    Kolinsky sable 24
    Nylon 26
    Ox hair 26
    Squirrel hair 26
Paint handling and storage 55
Paint, history of 8
Paint manufacture 9
Painting on plastics 52
Pantone 36
Paper masks 73
P.C.D. tape 70
Peaking 114
Pens 38
Perspex 15
Photocopy tricks 73
Pigment size 9
Plasticiser migration 94
Polyesters 17, 44
Polyester filling pastes 45
Polyfilla 43
Polykote 19
Polyurethane 19
Pop art 117
Power stirring 57
Precision paints 9
Preparation resins 45
Primers and fillers 41, 44
Refillable aerosols 36
Resin coating by roller 37
Robbe Argo 85
Rollers 37
Rotring 38

Rowney 15–25
Rub down lettering 76
Sanding sealer 42
Scotch clean art 71
Scotch spray mount 74
Self adhesive film trims 85
Sig epoxolite 45
Silicone release agents 48
Single action airbrushes 33
SOLARLAC 84
Solvent entrapment 59–62
Solvent evaporation 11
SP113 47
Spray guns 33
Spoke and rim lines 100
Stencil knives 75
Stippling brushes 79, 84
Stirring paint 56
Stoving paints 20
Superfiller 43
Super Smoothcote 42
Surface preparation 41
Swivel knife 75
Tape edge creep 88
Thinners 13
Tissue covering 42
Total suspension 55
Transparent car bodies (LEXAN) 94
Tufkote 23
Two pack paints 15, 17, 18, 19, 22
Viscosity 58–61
Water colours 21
Waterproof paints 91
Weathering 109
Weight saving 79
Wet line 98
Wet or dry paper 43
Wood/plastic finishing 53
Yacht varnish 19
Yellowing 99